TASTE
and
SEE

To Sally,
  Stephanie,
    and Diane

TASTE and SEE

A Personal Guide to the Spiritual Life

Revised Edition

William O. Paulsell

Wipf and Stock Publishers
EUGENE, OREGON

Wipf and Stock Publishers
199 West 8th Avenue, Suite 3
Eugene, Oregon 97401

Taste and See
A Personal Guide to the Spiritual Life
By Paulsell, William O.
©1992 Paulsell, William O.
ISBN: 1-57910-995-0
Publication date: June, 2002
Previously published by Chalice Press, 1992.

Contents

Introduction

As a deer longs for flowing streams,
so my soul longs for you, O God.
My soul thirsts for God,
for the living God.
When shall I come and behold
the face of God?

Psalm 42:1–2

Religion is our personal relationship with God. That is the essence of it. There are many things related to religion, but religion itself is simply a term that describes our experience with God and what we think it means. We can be moral without being religious; we can be socially concerned and responsible without being religious; we can be persons of compassion and goodwill without being religious. If there is no conscious communion with God there is no religion. Our church life, our morality, and our social activism are religious only if they are grounded in our experience with God. What makes us religious people is not the church we attend,

1

not the Bible we read, not even our good deeds. The only thing, finally, that makes us religious is our relationship with God.

This is a book of guidance on how to nurture and deepen that relationship. It is hoped that the ideas presented here will be helpful in making us more aware of God's presence in our lives and our status before the Divine. This book is very elementary, an introduction to the spiritual life. If we persevere and develop, we will move far beyond it. But here is a beginning. God is in the world, at work among us, loves us, and is constantly present in all of our experiences. Our problem is not that God is not here; our problem is that we are not aware of God. We have trouble discerning that mysterious Presence. We are distracted, anxious, and spiritually dry. The purpose of an intentional and disciplined devotional life is to open us, drive away the mist and darkness, and break down the barriers that restrict our perception of God.

A basic human problem is a tendency to ignore that our very existence, our whole being, and our destiny, depend upon the mercy and work of God. The world is here because God made it. God's sovereign power rules over all; no one can prevail against it. Why, then, do we live as if God were not really very important to us? Why do we not take the reality of God more seriously, turning to God only in time of crisis? We ought to give ourselves without reservation to the One who made us, but this is hard to do when we are unfamiliar with God, when our perception of God is blurred and shadowy.

If God is indeed sovereign, it is utter foolishness to ignore the One who is in complete control. Our lives cannot possibly be what they were intended to be apart from the Source of life. The folly of resisting the Power that transcends all human powers is so obvious that it is difficult to understand why we do it. Quite clearly, life can be what it should be only when it is lived in a conscious relationship with God.

Many spiritual writers have sensed the truth of this. St. Augustine wrote on the first page of his *Confessions* that we are restless until we rest in God. He sought satisfaction through learning, through fame, through sensuality, and through friendships, but he finally came to the conclusion that the only authentic satisfaction was to be found in God.

So our thesis is this: God is present. The purpose of any spiritual discipline is to help us recognize what is already a fact and open us up to the reality of God's presence in human life. The best life we can live is a life oriented toward God. To live any other way is to rebel against our Creator and to destroy what we were made to be. The ultimate goal of the spiritual or devotional life, as it will be described in this book, is to develop a deeper knowledge of God and to live as intimately with God as possible.

In these pages I will explain a number of practices that might be helpful. They are not magic formulas for instant spiritual experience, and their usefulness depends on our attitudes and desires more than anything else. These ideas are not even original. I have discovered them through studying the great Christian mystics and spiritual writers, through fruitful contacts with men and women of prayer whose lives are deeply contemplative, and through working with students and church members who are wrestling with their own spiritual problems. They have been tested by centuries of Christian experience. They include what, on the surface, would seem to be simple things: prayer, meditation, silence, certain kinds of reading, and a willingness to exercise self-discipline. They are not easy to maintain for an extended period of time, for a serious devotional life requires firm resolve, profound commitment, and a generous measure of the grace of God. But, if we will practice them we may become more open and receptive to God. They may help to sanctify our lives, sharpen our perceptions, and enable us to discern more clearly than before the work of God in the world.

A good bit has been written in this century expressing people's frustrations regarding a lack of clear evidence of the presence of God. It has been said that God is hidden, that God is in eclipse, even that God is dead. These statements may say more about people's lack of perception than they say about God.

Many individuals desire an experience with God that is so real, so ecstatic, and so convincing that there can be no doubt about what has happened. This has led to a renewed interest in Christian mysticism, a topic worthy of study by anyone seeking a deeper level of spiritual life. The classical mystical experience involves a union between the soul of the mystic and God. There are different levels of the experience, but this is the essence of it. Normally, it seems to come after a long period of rigorous self-discipline and spiritual training. Augustine, Bernard of Clairvaux, Meister Eckhart, Henry Suso, the unknown author of the *Cloud of Unknowing*, and John of the Cross are just a few of the better known examples of those who wrote about esoteric religious experiences and provided guidance for those seeking them.

My position in this book, however, is that mysticism or mystical religion does not have to mean esoteric experience. Our knowledge of God does not depend upon visions, ecstatic utterances, or strange feelings. In fact, many mystics see these things as obstacles. Rather, a mystical knowledge of God can result from an intensification of the ordinary Christian life. Deep religious experience grows out of an intense love of God and a steadily growing faith. There is nothing necessarily occult or exclusive about it. As we develop in the spiritual life we become increasingly aware of the presence and nature of God. This is not to say that the spiritual life has no struggle, pain, or discouragement. These problems will be discussed in Chapter 5. It is to say, however, that by orienting our lives toward God in a serious way, the presence of God in the world will become clearer to us.

Christianity advocates both horizontal and vertical relationships, and it seems that at various times in history one or the other has been emphasized. In recent years we have tended to place the emphasis on the horizontal relationships between people. We have urged love and concern for every individual; we have insisted on social justice; we have called for the building of more viable human communities; and we have sought to establish peace in the world. All of these are excellent expressions of the Christian ethic. They are what Jesus taught. But we must equally emphasize the vertical connection between God and human beings. This connection both motivates and helps us evaluate our horizontal relationships with each other.

Several years ago young people were showing a great interest in Eastern mystical traditions: Hinduism, Buddhism, and yoga. Some of this was a reaction to a brand of Christianity that defines religion as churchgoing, budget raising, and committee meeting. Even speculative theology runs a risk of being divisive chatter rather than a deep probing of the mystery of God. This kind of activity, no matter how well intentioned, misses the point. The Christian life, at the deepest level, is a life built firmly on an authentic and genuine relationship with God.

On a wall in front of the guest house of a famous American Trappist monastery, cast in concrete, are the words, "God alone." That summarizes the purpose of the lives of the monks who live there, and it expresses what ought to be the basic value for any Christian living anywhere. If we focus our lives on God alone, all of our activities and problems and hopes will begin to fit into place in a way that will make life more meaningful and clearly understood. One of the most important values of a deeper spiritual life is a sharpening of our perception of the nature of life, the world, and human relationships. It will help to drive away some of the fog and darkness so that we will come closer to seeing reality as it actually is.

This book, then, assumes that every Christian can develop a deeper experience of the presence of God and a fuller understanding of the divine mysteries. The fact that God is in the world is not very obvious on the superficial, surface level of human observation. To see it we must probe our experiences more deeply. True, we will always see in a mirror dimly until that day when we see face to face, but we must never stop the quest. If we ever think that we know all there is to know we condemn ourselves to the worst kind of spiritual stagnation. Progress and growth in the spiritual life come to those who can develop an increasing openness to God and what God chooses to reveal to us. The suggestions that follow are intended to help us create and nurture that openness.

It is a strange experience to revise a book one wrote eighteen years ago. I still stand by the original version, but have made a number of changes for this edition. Every effort has been made to use more inclusive language. Biblical quotations are taken from the New

Revised Standard Version without alteration. Chapter 7 is new and reflects an approach I did not understand until I began to study the spirituality of social activists. Minor revisions were made here and there to clarify ideas. An occasional sentence that might have been confusing or misleading has been deleted. In response to many questions I have received, a bibliography has been added. The basic intention of the book remains the same: to draw upon the classical history of Western Christian spirituality for ideas that might help us develop a deeper spiritual life.

There are many weaknesses in the book, the greatest being that it lacks a global dimension. Apart from some vague references to Eastern religions in general, Zen Buddhism in particular, and the Orthodox tradition, there is no discussion of non-Western or Third World spirituality. The study of spirituality in cultures other than our own can produce important insights and deepen our understanding of the God-human encounter. Additional projects await the future. Exploring ways that people encounter God in Latin America, Africa, Southeast Asia, India, and the Far East will be a fruitful study.

Beginning 1

O taste and see that the LORD is good;
happy are those who take refuge in
him.

Psalm 34:8

A college student on retreat at a religious community asked the Guestmaster, a wise man of deep faith and broad experience, how he could find time to pray on a regular basis when he returned to his campus. The Guestmaster replied, "How badly do you want to do it?" That is the only answer to a question like that. One of the easiest tasks in life is finding excuses for not doing something. There are many good reasons for neglecting devotional activity: We are too busy, our jobs are too demanding, our families require all our spare time, and we are physically exhausted when all the things we have to do each day are done.

There is only one good reason for deepening ourselves spiritually. It is expressed well in Psalm 34, which speaks of tasting and seeing that the Lord is good and of finding that happiness that comes when we take refuge in God. If we seriously want to know God and live in communion with the Divine, the excuses lose their force and somehow we find a way and a time to develop that openness that will enable us to "taste and see that the Lord is good."

There are several prerequisites necessary to the development of a strong devotional life. Of course, in the beginning they will not be fully perfected; that is a lifelong process. But they must exist to some degree before any significant progress can be made.

The first of these must be *desire*. Getting into serious prayer will be frustrating and painful enough if we have a strong desire to do so. It will be hopeless if we just go through the motions because we think that this is what a Christian is supposed to do. Only when we are willing to take seriously the idea that we can understand life better if we understand God better will we have a deep enough desire to embark on a fruitful spiritual pilgrimage. In a later chapter more will be said about facing the frustrations of the spiritual life. For now it is enough to say that they will be enormous. Only a serious desire to taste and see will be able to carry us through the difficult times.

As Jesus explained in the parable of the sower, the gospel bears fruit only on properly cultivated soil. If a serious desire is lacking, there may be a few quick spurts of growth, but the plant will die. Spirituality is not something faddish to play around with. No spiritual teacher or method is going to provide instant mystical union with God or immediate religious satisfaction. There is no magic formula that will suddenly drive away all mystery.

Jesus said that the first and greatest commandment is to love God. There marks the real beginning of the spiritual life. It is our love for God that moves us to want to taste and see, to search out the divine mysteries. But it is hard to love God if we do not know God.

This problem was dealt with by a great spiritual teacher who lived in twelfth-century France. He is known in history as Bernard of Clairvaux. He was the abbot of a famous monastery, he was a preacher of unsurpassed ability, he was active in European affairs of church and state, and he was a mystic. One of his most famous writings is a little treatise called *On Loving God*. Bernard described our love for God as developing through four steps. First, we love ourselves. That is where we all begin. Before we love anything or anyone else, we love ourselves. Second, we love God because of all that God does for us. We realize that there are some things we cannot do for ourselves, and we love God for doing them for us. Third, we move beyond selfishness and love God simply because God is God. Having taken our petitions to God time after time, we have gradually developed a more intimate relationship. We have begun to taste and see and no longer worry about what God might do for us. We love God for God's own sake. The fourth step, which Bernard doubted could take place in this life, involves loving ourselves because we belong to God. We no longer love ourselves except for God's sake; we no longer will or desire anything except that which God wants.

The point of Bernard's analysis is that progress in the spiritual life feeds desire. The more steps we take, the more knowledge we uncover, the more we will want to seek the next level and penetrate more deeply into the mystery. And the more we will love God as our relationship becomes more intimate and real.

In preparing to begin a serious devotional life, then, we must have a strong desire to know and experience the reality of God. This may be stimulated in many ways. We may realize our position in the cosmos as creatures that live under the sovereign power of God and want to understand this power more deeply. We may, as a result of deep theological speculation, want to experience that Divinity whom theologians have struggled to explain and define. We may read the lives and experiences of great saints and mystics and desire what they have found, a knowledge of God that produced confidence and certainty. Or, best of all, we may simply want to taste and see that the Lord is. Whatever pushes us, little significant progress will be made apart from a strong desire.

A second essential element in the quest for spiritual development is an *openness to God.* Strong conviction on religious matters is an admirable quality, but it can be dangerous if it closes our minds to a point of view or an idea where God just might reveal something to us. One of the dangerous tendencies of modern life is a desire to categorize people. In politics, economics, education, religion, or almost any other field, we tend to regard a person as liberal or conservative, radical or moderate, left or right, orthodox or heretic. Once we have chosen our own stance we tend to regard all others as in error. We might be closing our minds to something God is revealing to us.

Each of the major Christian traditions has contributed something important to the development of human understanding of God. Roman Catholicism preserved the gospel in Western civilization for over a thousand years. Lutheranism rediscovered the ancient Pauline doctrine of justification by faith. Calvinism stressed the majesty and sovereignty of God. Methodism emphasized heartfelt religious piety. Baptists promoted vigorous evangelism. Disciples stressed a rational approach to religion. God has been at work in all of these movements and many others, and we must be open to the leading of the Holy Spirit, wherever it may be and wherever it may take us.

It would be well for us to remember that we are not saved by doctrine or theological positions; we are saved by the mercy of God. People's efforts to understand and explain God have had only limited success, at best. It would be arrogant indeed to assert that only we know the truth about God when there seems to be so little that God reveals to us. But worse than that, any egocentric position may well cut us off from knowledge and truth that could deepen our religious awareness.

Doctrine and creed are important, but they are only attempts at verbal expressions of God's inexpressible love. Only the love of God has saving power, and we must be open to any legitimate expression of it, traditional or nontraditional. We must avoid the danger of saying no to something that God may be using for self-revelation.

A young man about to enter military service told me that he was advised by an older brother to get the most out of every situation in which he would find himself. This advice was taken, and the man was promoted through the ranks in the minimum amount of time possible. That is good advice for the spiritual life, too. We must draw all we can from the riches of the whole Christian experience: medieval mysticism, the Protestant Reformation, the Social Gospel, evangelical piety, and the struggles of theologians. All have something to add to our religious knowledge, and this additional understanding can deepen and broaden our religious experience. The more open we allow ourselves to be, the more progress we will make. God is present in our lives. If we are not aware of this fact, it is because we are not sufficiently open to see it.

A third requirement for beginning a deeper spiritual life is *self-discipline*. The following three chapters contain discussions of various aspects of mental self-discipline, the most difficult kind. But other forms of it are required of us, too.

The Christian tradition is full of stories of saints and mystics who practiced extreme forms of self-denial: fasting, poverty, flagellation, going without sleep or bodily comforts. Such accounts seem rather quaint and irrelevant in modern times. It is generally true, however, that an undisciplined life accomplishes little of permanent or lasting value. Whether one is an athlete, an artist, a scientist, or a successful businessperson, some self-discipline must be exercised. Some things must be denied, at least temporarily, for the sake of achieving a more important goal. We do not need to wear hair shirts, but we do need to take seriously the spirit of self-discipline.

Our perception of God is often obstructed by our attachment to things that have nothing to do with God. The reason most mystics have regarded poverty as a virtue is that they did not want anything to distract them from the vision of God. Possessing things is no vice; it only becomes a problem for us if we take it too seriously. Obviously, if our main goals in life consist only of always driving the latest model automobile or always wearing the latest fashions, our spiritual life is going to be pretty superficial. If we could be generally indifferent to such things so long as our lifestyle is not offensive to those we would influence, we would be much freer to pursue matters of ultimate and transcendent importance.

Christian mystical writers have frequently said that the less we are attached to created things in the world the better we are able to discern the presence of God. It is a question of values. If we genuinely seek God alone we do not have to worry about self-denial. We will naturally tend to take less seriously those things that do not contribute to a deepening of our religious experience. Self-denial for its own sake is just as bad as overindulgence. We miss the whole point if we fall into the trap of taking pride in what we have given up for the sake of our religion.

Nevertheless, a decision to live a deeper spiritual life involves a willingness to practice some degree of self-discipline. We will not make much progress spiritually if we indulge every appetite whenever we feel like it. A life that is slovenly physically will probably be slovenly spiritually. To probe the depths of the mysteries of God we must be alert and free. We must minimize our dependence upon things and maximize our orientation toward God.

We will, of course, never be completely free to pursue the knowledge of God. The problem of physical survival cannot be ignored. Responsibilities must be met. But there is much that is trivial and unimportant that we can cast off from our lives. We do not need all the things an acquisitive society would persuade us we need.

One of the obvious characteristics of the great mystics and spiritual teachers in Christian history was simplicity of life. Wherever possible they simplified things and gave no attention to the superficial, the petty, the unimportant, or the nonessential. As a preparation for a deeper spiritual life, then, we will need to reorder some priorities and simplify our lives as much as is practicable, knowing that many things we think we have to be concerned about distract us from our perception of God. We need to seek out and attach ourselves to that which will aid us in our religious quest.

A fourth basic requirement for beginning the spiritual life is *an understanding of the essence of the gospel.* The sovereign God under whose absolute power we live is a God of love and mercy. Our relationship with God, our destiny, our immortality, are all gifts. Our status before God no longer depends on obedience to religious law, it depends upon the love of God which has been revealed to us in Jesus Christ, a love that is forgiving and redemptive.

As far as the spiritual life is concerned, this means that we can know God only because God has taken the initiative of self-revelation. There is hope for success in our spiritual quest because God does come into human experience. Remember the admonition of Azariah to Asa in the Old Testament, "The LORD is with you, while you are with him. If you seek him, he will be found by you" (2 Chronicles 15:2). The apostle Paul told the Romans that God helps people in their spiritual development and overcomes even their inability to pray. "Likewise the Spirit helps us in our weakness; for we do not know how to pray as we ought, but that very Spirit intercedes with sighs too deep for words. And God, who searches the heart, knows what is the mind of the Spirit, because the Spirit intercedes for the saints according to the will of God" (Romans 8:26–27).

There are many things we can do to foster the spiritual life. We can pray, we can meditate, we can read scripture, we can study theology. All of these will deepen our understanding of God, but there will eventually come a time when, having done them all to the limits of our abilities, we must simply turn the whole effort over to God and trust in God's mercy. The knowledge of God is, after all, a gift of grace. Spiritual progress is possible only because God is willing to draw back the veil and be disclosed to us. Trusting in our own efforts, taking pride in our own piety, will lead to frustration and failure. Having faith in the mercy of God opens us up and makes us receptive to the divine presence.

These, then, are some elementary prerequisites for beginning a deeper spiritual and devotional life and a more serious quest for a knowledge of and experience with God. We must have a strong desire for God, we must be open to all possible sources of truth, we must be willing to exercise self-discipline in avoiding distractions, and we must understand our dependence upon the grace and mercy of God.

But, let me hasten to add that a religious person cannot be expected to possess all of these qualities in their fullest at the beginning. That would be a naive and unrealistic expectation. Rather, these are tendencies or points of view we must begin to accept. As we proceed in our quest, they will be developed and perfected. Our desire for God may increase as our experience with God deepens. We cannot really know what it means to be open until we learn something from a totally unexpected source. If we make significant progress we will find that our lives are becoming more disciplined. And, if we grow in prayer, we will understand the meaning of the gospel on a more profound level.

So, let us begin.

Silence

2

For God alone my soul waits in silence;
from him comes my salvation.
He alone is my rock and my salvation,
my fortress; I shall never be shaken.

Psalm 62:1–2

Silence is absolutely essential to the spiritual life. Very little in the way of deep progress can take place without it. Modern people seem frightened of it and go to great lengths to avoid it. Piped in music is everywhere. We even have to listen to it when we are put on hold on the telephone. Few people would own an automobile without a radio or stereo tape or CD player. Most of our homes have some kind of electronic device available to combat silence. We will watch the most inane television programs just to have something to do, to avoid silence.

Silence is difficult to find these days. The steady flow of noise moving through our daily lives almost overwhelms us. Industry, entertainment, transportation, our friends, all bombard us with noise. Even the church is guilty. Quiet moments, when no one is speaking in a worship service, are usually filled with music so that we do not have to sit in silence and face the reality of God. The various interludes as the service progresses, times of silent prayer, the serving of the Lord's Supper, the receiving of an offering, are usually filled with music and song. No one wants to face pure silence. Yet, if we seriously want to contemplate the reality of God we must minimize distractions. We must remove as many things as possible that would divert our attention from focusing upon God. There are times when the church must stop providing us with information and performances and let us search for God in the depths of silence. But if we are going to do this, we need to learn how to use silence profitably.

A young man I know, who had held a variety of jobs after graduating from high school, became attracted to the Christian ministry as a possible life's work. He went off by himself for three days to think it over. Later, he told me that the silence was a terrible problem. All sorts of unwanted thoughts came into his mind, and he kept thinking about difficult questions for which there seemed to be no answers.

There are dangers in silence. Jesus encountered Satan in the silence of the wilderness. But, using silence constructively is one of the major disciplines we must develop. The Trappist monk kneeling motionless in his monastery chapel for a long period of time and the Zen Buddhist sitting in a lotus position have one thing in common: They are sufficiently disciplined that they are using their silence in highly constructive ways. Their minds are not wandering nor are they daydreaming.

I received a letter from a woman living in a small experimental community of families devoted to prayer and contemplation. The people worked to provide for their material needs, but their main purpose was prayer and seeking a more profound awareness of God. She mentioned in her letter that people often came by to look over the community, but that group visits were discouraged. "It's easy to talk about prayer," she wrote, "easier than being alone and having to get on with it." Silence forces us to get on with it. We are compelled to come to terms with our own condition while we are particularly conscious of the presence of God. We can, of course, mentally run away from the situation, but in doing so we lose a marvelous opportunity for struggle and growth.

An important use of silence is for what spiritual directors call *recollection*. This refers to using silence as a means of preparation for worship, receiving communion, prayer, or meditation. Recollection is a matter of clearing out the mental clutter and pushing aside the distractions. In involves developing an openness to God. It is not easy to do, and the harder we try the more impossible it seems. It takes real practice and effort, but it is important that we gain as much control as possible over our mental processes. Finally, however, we must remember that an awareness of God is finally a gift of grace. Our task is to develop an openness to grace.

As difficult as this is, we can meditate and pray much better if we are prepared. Trying to rush into an awareness of the presence of God and hurriedly offering up prayers or meditating on some religious theme is not going to be very profitable. It may be the best we can do for the moment and may be better than nothing, but it is not likely to produce any deep religious growth. We must take our time, not hurry, and prepare our minds in silence before we begin to struggle with the great mysteries. Then we will be much more receptive and ready for insight.

Under the most ideal conditions we should sit in a comfortable position, yet not so comfortable that we might become drowsy. The goal is to relax and think of nothing. At first, all sorts of thoughts will rush into our minds: the events of the day, persistent long-term worries, short-term obligations that must soon be met, things we will do in the future, and unpleasant thoughts we do not want but that seem to torment us from time to time. If we have set for ourselves a given period of time for silence, we can deal with these thoughts to some extent by realizing that there is nothing we can do about them for the moment. We can always return to them later.

These random thoughts dance on the surface of our minds. When we withdraw deeper into silence they will be less of a problem and our mental activity will gradually run down. As beginners we must not push ourselves too hard. Rather, let the mind slowly come to rest. Our breathing should slow a little as we become increasingly relaxed.

It is difficult for a beginner to focus attention on nothingness, and it is often useful to have something simple to look at or think about. A candle flame, a devotional object such as a cross, or a simple design might help. These things should not be taken too seriously, however. They are only means to help us focus and should be dropped when they are no longer useful. Nevertheless, by concentrating our attention on one very simple thing the other thoughts in our minds will fade away. Approach this gently; don't get a headache by trying too hard. The fewer thoughts we have cluttering our consciousness, the more open we will be to God.

Focusing on a physical object outside the mind might not work successfully for everyone. Students of Zen Buddhism concentrate on counting breaths, starting at twenty, for example, and counting backward. Doing this several times, for some people, induces a state of relaxation and calm in which silence becomes a rich experience.

Another possibility would be to fill our minds with one simple thought. This would have the effect of excluding all others. A simple verse of scripture would do, something like "God is love," or "Jesus Christ is Lord," or "The Lord is my shepherd." This brings us to a technique used in a number of religions, the use of a mantra. *Mantra* is a Sanskrit word meaning "instrument of thought." It is a word or phrase or a syllable of invocation that is repeated over and over. The repetitive use of a mantra is supposed to produce insight and open our minds to transcendence. Some people have even claimed mystical union through using it.

Transcendental Meditation, which was popular several years ago, was based on the use of a mantra that, in theory, was specifically designed for each individual. Practitioners reported that the meditative repetition of their mantra for twenty minutes twice each day produced better health, more energy, and a general sense of well-being. However, our interest here is not in psychological exercises, but in practices that help us probe the mystery of God.

A similar devotional method has appeared in Christianity throughout the history of the church. One example, which comes from Eastern Orthodox Christianity and which will be explained more fully in Chapter 4, is the so-called Jesus Prayer. Orthodox monks would repeat over and over, thousands of times a day, the simple prayer, "Lord Jesus Christ, Son of God, have mercy on me a sinner." A classic devotional book of anonymous authorship from the fourteenth century, *The Cloud of Unknowing,* urged constant focusing on one word as a way of maintaining an awareness of God's presence. For centuries, Roman Catholics have repeated the "Hail Mary" as each bead of a rosary is counted. People in the Pentecostal movement today often repeat the name of Jesus in prayer. The basic idea is that the word or phrase is to be repeated in rhythm with our breathing so that it becomes a natural part of our living.

How deeply we might want to go into this practice will depend upon our experience with it. Minimally, however, it could help us calm ourselves or "center down" as many spiritual writers put it. There is nothing magic here. We are simply talking about a mental discipline and a way of prayer that can help us ease into silence and profit from it.

Once we become used to genuine interior silence we will covet it and seek it out often. A clear mind has so much more freedom than a cluttered one. For many years I have been retreating in a monastery that begins the day in the middle of the night, at 3:00 a.m. There are many reasons for this, but one is that it is a time of deep quiet. The world is asleep, everything is still, there are no disruptions. It is the favorite time for many monks. It is a time when it is easy to pray, easy to sense the presence of God. The day's work has not yet begun, and the mind is clear and free.

Having developed to some degree the art of achieving interior silence, what are we to do with it? For one thing, we will learn to relish the freedom of it. We should find it refreshing. It is basic preparation for any kind of devotional activity. If we could experience it before public worship on Sunday morning, we would probably find ourselves more receptive to what happens there. People who complain that Sunday morning church services are lifeless and dull probably do not prepare themselves for such occasions. They rush in at the last minute expecting a performance that will entertain them and hold their attention, and if it does not turn out that way they regard the hour as wasted. Yet something is happening when the word of God is read and proclaimed and the sacraments administered. If we prepare ourselves with silence and cleanse our minds of extraneous thoughts, we will be much more receptive to the revelation of God to us. When we enter church expectantly, alert, and prepared for an encounter with God, something will happen and we will receive insight that will deepen our faith.

The same kind of preparation is important for reading scripture devotionally. Martin Luther said that we might read the words of the Bible and never actually encounter the word of God. We must sharpen our perception by sound interior preparation so that when we read or hear scripture we will recognize the Word in the words. And, of course, this is true of any kind of devotional reading. Spiritual growth cannot be rushed; we progress by steps. But it is necessary that we make some of the progress in silence.

Solitude and silence, however, are not ends in themselves. They are preparation for more fruitful contact with the world. In attempting to develop the devotional life we ought to use Jesus as our model. For example, read Luke 5:12–16. Jesus healed a leper. Almost immediately a huge crowd gathered; many people presented themselves to Jesus for healing. But what did he do on such occasions? "He would withdraw to deserted places and pray."

No one could accuse Jesus of neglecting human need or not being concerned about suffering humanity. But Jesus recognized the need for periodic withdrawal for prayer, for renewal, for communion with God. Withdrawal into silence helps us recover our equilibrium and perspective. It gives us time to renew and reset our goals.

There are probably more opportunities for growth through silence than we realize. We may not find many around the house when others need our attention, but possibilities are nearby. Taking a walk alone, even around the backyard, may provide us with some silence and solitude. An important part of the Christian ascetic tradition has been manual labor. People devoting their lives to prayer have found quiet, boring work, the kind that requires very little thought, to be conducive to the spiritual life. I once knew a weaver who kept a little flip chart of three-by-five cards on his loom. On each card was written a passage of scripture or a quotation from some spiritual classic. These were food for meditation while the monotonous weaving was being done. Even simple chores, like yard work or gardening, can be opportunities for quiet and solitude if we approach them with the right attitude. Frequently, when traveling by plane or bus we are alone, and, even though we may be in a crowd, the fact that we are among strangers can produce some useful solitude.

One factor that can help us find more opportunities for silence is simplicity of life. The busier we are the more difficult it is to find quiet times. Here again, the question of values arises. Are all the things that demand our time and energy really that important? Are we indispensable to all the clubs, organizations, and groups in which we work? Are all the things we get ourselves involved in actually that useful and necessary

to our families and our communities? The answers to
these questions will become clearer as we progress in
our spiritual development. But sooner or later we have
to face the fact that to taste and see that the Lord is good
we must engage in some withdrawal and begin the
development of the interior life. We have to find that
silence where we can be still and know God.

Meditation 3

Great are the works of the LORD,
studied by all who delight in them.

Psalm 111:2

One of the basic tools for spiritual growth is meditation. It is also one of the most difficult. It takes considerable self-discipline. Almost anyone can exert enough willpower to avoid food, sleep, or other pleasures for at least a short period of time, but pondering one topic for even a few minutes without letting the mind wander is considerably more difficult. Most of us probably have more control over our bodies than we have over our minds. Serious meditation is not easy, but the potential rewards are great. As in all things in the spiritual life, our quest is encouraged and aided by God's grace.

There are many approaches to meditation. For our purposes here we will define it as directing our thoughts toward God in a systematic manner. Meditation involves the mental examination of those things that will help to deepen our understanding of the divine mystery. Focusing our thoughts on one idea for an extended period of time can produce insight and a more mature understanding of religious reality. Some spiritual writers have reported meditating on one verse of scripture for months, even years, and of discerning truth that a surface examination had never revealed.

One of the more interesting developments in modern Christian spirituality is a new openness to meditative methods from Eastern religions. There is much to be learned that will enrich our Christian faith. The human quest for the Divine is universal, and it is foolish not to examine the insights others have discovered. One Eastern tradition about which there has been much interest and writing on the part of Christians is Zen Buddhism. That approach to meditation involves sitting in silence, thinking about nothing, in the hope of improving clarity of vision and achieving enlightenment.

The style of meditation to be discussed here, however, involves imaging, focusing our attention on scripture, and probing it as a guide to our own experience.

There are many benefits to be gained from meditation. A number of knowledgeable people believe that regular meditation produces better general health, sharper perception, a more pleasant disposition, and longer life. Some people engage in various forms of meditation to reap these particular benefits. For the Christian, however, such benefits are of minimal relevance and importance. If they accrue, that is fine, but Christians seeking to make spiritual progress enter into meditation as a means of deepening our understanding of and intimacy with God. It is in this context that meditation will be discussed here.

It must be understood, however, that meditation is not just an intellectual exercise. It involves the whole person: body, mind, and heart. We are not just thinking, we are also loving. Speculating about the nature of God will not produce the kind of spiritual growth we have been discussing here if it is not done in love. To be sure, our love for God is imperfect, but as our meditation deepens, our love for God will also deepen. So, as we concentrate our thoughts on God, we also direct all of our love to God. Without this element, our meditation will be nothing more than academic speculation.

The previous chapter on silence described the necessary preparation for meditation. The mind must be cleared. Extraneous thoughts must be put aside temporarily. We must get into a physical position where we are reasonably comfortable but alert. Having relaxed the mind and body, we are next faced with the question of a subject for meditation. The options are almost limitless, but for a beginning let us consider the Bible as a possibility. We can take a particular passage, examine it, ponder it, and think about many possible meanings of it.

The Bible contains many types of material, some of them useful for meditation, some of them not. Certain chapters in the books of Numbers and Leviticus, for example, are not particularly inspiring. Neither are the genealogies in Matthew and Luke, although some people have found meditative value in them. Some of the cursing Psalms might cause problems, at least in the beginning.

Many parts of the Bible, however, lend themselves well to the kind of meditation I have described. The majority of the Psalms and most of the Gospels would make good beginning points. Serious meditation on this kind of material could produce an intense deepening of the spiritual life.

There are many ways to read the Bible. A well-trained scholar might read it with an eye for textual problems, historical information, the use of theological terms, literary forms, cultural accretions, and the usages of Hebrew or Greek. A theologian might read it with an interest in doctrinal questions. A minister might study it for preaching material. All of these elements are important to anyone wanting to deepen spiritually, for an intelligent knowledge of the Bible is essential for spiritual growth.

It is a somewhat different matter to read the Bible devotionally and meditatively. Here we do not consciously deal with technical questions, although we will be aware of them as we approach the Bible, and they will have shaped our thinking about a passage. Our purpose now is to let the scriptures engage us and stimulate our spiritual growth. We seek to be challenged by the biblical tradition as we work with a specific passage. We will turn it over in our minds, apply it to our experience, compare it with other religious ideas we have encountered, and probe deeply into its content.

An excellent place to begin using scripture meditatively is the Psalms in the Old Testament, the prayer book of the Bible. Dietrich Bonhoeffer, the German theologian martyred by the Nazis near the end of World War II, wrote that he read the Psalms every day. Martin Luther, the father of Protestantism, said that the whole gospel could be found in the Psalms. In his own *Preface to the Psalter*, published in 1534, Luther wrote, "In short, would you see the Holy Christian Church painted with living colour and form, fastened together in one picture, take your Psalter, and you have a fine, clear, pure mirror which will show you what Christianity is." Luther had been an Augustinian monk, and in Christian monasteries, down through the centuries, the daily chanting of the Psalms had formed the basis of the community prayer life. The Psalms were the praises of ancient Israel, and they became the hymnbook of the early church.

There are many kinds of Psalms—praise, thanksgiving, penance, petition, enthronement, and vengeance. The full range of human experience is touched upon, and in this book we find people at their best and at their worst. In one psalm God is asked to demolish a people with the sword. In another, the psalmist soars to the loftiest heights of mystical aspiration. For example, compare these two passages:

> Rise up, O LORD!
> Deliver me, O my God!
> For you strike all my enemies on the
>   cheek;
>   you break the teeth of the wicked.
> Psalm 3:7

> As a deer longs for flowing streams,
>   so my soul longs for you, O God.
> My soul thirsts for God,
>   for the living God.
> Psalm 42:1–2

Bitter feelings of vengeance and deep religious longings are both expressed here.

The songs in the Psalter are there because they expressed the most profound religious feelings of the people of Israel, even though some of these feelings might not be virtuous by Christian standards. They all expressed the idea that God does intervene in the affairs of the world to assist the just and the penitent.

One of the best devotional disciplines is to read the Psalms with regularity. Most people should be able to cover the entire Psalter in a month or less by reading only fifteen minutes a day. One of the values in becoming familiar with the Psalms is that they gradually become our own prayers. When we meditate on the Psalms with regularity we find that they express our own thoughts, concerns, and feelings.

There are many systems for classifying Psalms into various categories, but the problem with this is that we tend to read those kinds of Psalms that we like and ignore those we find difficult to interpret. We would do better to become intimately acquainted with all the Psalms, for each one has something important to express about the relationship between ourselves and God.

Many of the Psalms describe our own religious longings, and we can easily identify with them.

> Turn, O Lord! How long?
> Have compassion on your servants!
> Satisfy us in the morning with your
>   steadfast love,
>   so that we may rejoice and be glad
>   all our days.
>   Psalm 90:13–14

> My God, my God, why have you
>   forsaken me?
> Why are you so far from helping
>   me, from the words of my
>   groaning?

> O my God, I cry by day, but you do not
>   answer;
> and by night, but find no rest.
> Psalm 22:1–2

Most of us, from time to time, have felt abandoned
by God, and the frustrations expressed in these verses
are emotions with which we can easily identify. At the
same time, they express the conviction that life is
nothing without God. As we meditate carefully on
passages like these we begin to see the truth of that
affirmation, and the pleading of the psalmist becomes
our own pleading.

In other Psalms we find the same affirmation, but
with a more positive hope.

> For God alone my soul waits in silence,
>   for my hope is in him.
> He alone is my rock and my salvation,
>   my fortress, I shall not be shaken.
> Psalm 62:5–6

Psalms of penance constitute another important
group. The classical example is Psalm 51, a psalm David
was supposed to have prayed after the affair with
Bathsheba.

> Have mercy on me, O God,
>   according to your steadfast love;
> according to your abundant mercy
>   blot out my transgressions.
> Wash me thoroughly from my iniquity,
>   and cleanse me from my sin.
> Psalm 51:1–2

Meditation on this kind of psalm not only helps us to
make our own confessions to God, but instills within us

a deeper sense of the seriousness of our offenses against God.

The Psalms are filled with prayers of petition. Meditation on them ultimately leads to the conclusion that the only source of help that means anything at all is God.

> Do not forsake me, O LORD;
>   O my God, do not be far from me;
> make haste to help me,
>   O Lord, my salvation.
>
> Psalm 38:21–22

Sometimes the petition is a request for deeper religious knowledge.

> Make me to know your ways, O LORD;
>   teach me your paths.
> Lead me in your truth, and teach me,
>   for you are the God of my salvation;
>   for you I wait all day long.
>
> Psalm 25:4–5

On other occasions there is a general request for protection.

> Protect me, O God, for in you I take
>   refuge.
>
> Psalm 16:1

> O LORD, God of my salvation,
>   when, at night, I cry out in your
>   presence,
> let my prayer come before you;
>   incline your ear to my cry.
>
> Psalm 88:1–2

The most difficult Psalms to interpret are those that ask for the enemy to be destroyed. In the light of Jesus' admonition to love our enemies this passage seems strangely inappropriate:

Do I not hate those who hate you, O LORD?
And do I not loathe those who rise up
against you?
I hate them with perfect hatred;
I count them my enemies.

Psalm 139:21–22

Psalm 109 is probably the harshest of all the Psalms. The psalmist expressed bitter feelings toward an enemy.

May his days be few;
may another seize his position.
May his children be orphans,
and his wife a widow.
May his children wander about and
beg;
may they be driven out of the ruins
they inhabit.
May the creditor seize all that he has;
may strangers plunder the fruits of
his toil.
May there be no one to do him a
kindness,
nor anyone to pity his orphaned
children.

Psalm 109:8–12

These are not the kinds of sentiments that are devotionally beneficial. In fact, they are contrary to the virtues the gospel teaches. How are we to deal with them? The question cannot be ignored by anyone who would attempt to meditate on the Psalms and use them as prayer.

It may be that nothing helpful can be said about these kinds of Psalms. They certainly do not reflect the teachings of Jesus that we must love our enemies and do good to those who persecute us. On the face of it, Christians must reject these sentiments. They are neither edifying nor virtuous.

But they are part of Christian scripture, and for that reason we must come to terms with them. Two things can be said. First of all, even though they are in scripture, there is a sense in which they are not so much God's word to us as our word to God. They express the psalmists' bitter resentments. Before we become too judgmental, we might consider whether we have ever experienced hatred for another, even to the point of wanting to see that person suffer serious misfortune. If not toward an individual, have we ever had these feelings toward an enemy of our church or nation or freedom? Our own problems of hatred are not unique; at least some of the writers of the Psalms struggled with the same emotions. If anything, these Psalms reveal that we can identify with the psalmists in their humanity as well as in their lofty religious aspirations. They expose the dark side of ourselves and force us to face it.

A second point to be considered, however, is that these cursing Psalms affirm a strong belief in God's absolute opposition to evil, and that is clearly a legitimate topic for meditation. God forgives people, according to the gospel, but that does not lessen God's opposition to evil. The psalmists identified all who did evil as the enemies of God. The dangers in regarding our personal enemies as God's enemies are obvious, but at least when meditating on these psalms of vengeance and anger, we can recognize that God does oppose evil. We can also empathize with the hope that God will act to destroy evil in people's lives. This is the ultimate Christian hope.

> Rise up, O God, judge the earth;
> for all the nations belong to you!
>   Psalm 82:8

There is a long tradition of biblical interpretation that dates back to the early church fathers that tended to see certain passages of scripture as allegories of the spiritual life. There are dangers in this approach to the Bible, the greatest of which is to read into the biblical text what was never intended by the writers. But, if used with care and integrity, there are some helpful possibilities here, particularly in interpreting the Psalms.

For example, we might think of the various enemies condemned in the Psalms as enemies of the spiritual life such as pride, laziness, selfishness, and hatred. We all need God's help in destroying these interior foes. Apply this interpretation to the first two verses of Psalm 3.

> O LORD, how many are my foes!
> Many are rising against me;
> many are saying to me,
> "There is no help for you in God."

We know that there are many foes within us that would keep us from God: ambition, material desires, resentments toward others, concern for ourselves above all else. All of these traits rise up against us and try to convince us that there is no help to be had from God.

Even a passage such as "May his children wander about and beg," from Psalm 109 can be understood allegorically. All of our sins produce children. Pride, for instance, gives birth to alienation, suspicion, arrogance, and prejudice. These are children we hope will perish and be driven from the ruins they inhabit. Such interpretations must be faithful to the gospel and in continuity with the general sense of biblical truth. We must not push this approach too far and read all kinds of fantasy in the text, but it can be useful in meditating on the cursing Psalms.

God is sovereign over all creation. Nothing is beyond the range of God's power. When a Psalm asks God for the destruction of the enemy, it is asking God to exercise sovereign power and destroy evil. One problem we must keep in mind, however, is that when we ask God to destroy injustice, arrogance, selfishness, or other forms of evil, we might well be praying about the sin in our own lives.

This leads us to another important devotional practice that will be discussed in more detail later, the examination of conscience. How honest are our intentions? Psalm 78 is a lengthy song about the faithlessness of Israel. Does it describe our own faithlessness?

> They remembered that God was their
>   rock,
>   the Most High God their redeemer.
> But they flattered him with their
>   mouths;
>   they lied to him with their tongues.
>   Psalm 78:35–36

It is one thing to pray; it is something else to pray honestly and with integrity. A careful examination of the motives behind our prayers is essential, as the Psalms remind us.

Many of the Psalms describe the virtues of the righteous and are useful for self-evaluation.

> They have distributed freely,
>   they have given to the poor;
> their righteousness endures forever;
>   their horn is exalted in honor.
>   Psalm 112:9

Happy are those who do not follow the
advice of the wicked,
or take the path that sinners tread,
or sit in the seat of scoffers;
but their delight is in the law of the
LORD,
and on his law they meditate day
and night.

Psalm 1:1–2

O LORD, who may abide in your tent?
Who may dwell on your holy hill?
Those who walk blamelessly, and do
what is right,
and speak the truth from their
heart;
who do not slander with their tongue
and do no evil to their friends,
nor take up a reproach against
their neighbors.

Psalm 15:1–3

The admonition to examine our consciences is im-
plied in Psalm 139 where the psalmist acknowledges
that God examines them anyway.

O LORD, you have searched me and
known me.
You know when I sit down and
when I rise up;
you discern my thoughts from far
away.
You search out my path and my lying
down,
and are acquainted with all my
ways.

> Even before a word is on my tongue,
>   O Lord, you know it completely.
> > > Psalm 139:1–4

What excellent help these psalms give us for evaluating ourselves. Meditating on them can be a great benefit in forming our lives.

One more category of Psalms useful for meditation is that of praise and thanksgiving. Many of the Psalms are devoted to the praise of God under whose sovereignty we live and in whose grace we hope.

> The Lord is my light and my salvation;
>   whom shall I fear?
> The Lord is the stronghold of my life,
>   of whom shall I be afraid?
> > > Psalm 27:1–2

> Bless the Lord, O my soul,
>   and all that is within me,
>   bless his holy name.
> Bless the Lord, O my soul,
>   and do not forget all his benefits.
> > > Psalm 103:1–2

> Praise the Lord!
>   O give thanks to the Lord, for he is
>   good;
>   for his steadfast love endures
>   forever.
> > > Psalm 106:1

> Great are the works of the Lord,
>   studied by all who delight in them.
> Full of honor and majesty is his work
>   and his righteousness endures
>   forever.
> > > Psalm 111:2–3

The Psalms cover a wide range of human experience and emotion and constitute a wealth of ideas for meditation. Regular meditation on them will lead us into serious thoughts on both our own religious longings and the ways of God with people. They will gradually become our own prayers. If we take these ancient songs seriously we cannot help but become lost in the mystery of God, that mystery in which they were composed, and in that condition the reality of God will become clearer to us.

A second basic source for meditative material is the life of Jesus as presented in the New Testament. The early church taught the gospel, in part, by retelling the life of Jesus. God was incarnate in Jesus Christ, and as we come to understand his life, we come to understand the nature of God.

God is spirit. No physical object can adequately represent the Divine. God is invisible, infinite, and incorporeal. That is why no visible thing can be regarded as holy. Nothing is holy but God. At the deepest level of spiritual development we think of God without the use of any mental images.

But this is virtually impossible, for most of us cannot think in terms of pure abstraction. We find it very difficult to contemplate God as spirit. We would rather think of God as an elderly person with a long beard, seated on a golden throne resting on a cloud. But we know this is a childish description of an infinite God who is omnipotent, omniscient, omnipresent, and ineffable.

The gospel teaches us that Jesus was more than just a good person; he was one in whom God was incarnate. God was in Christ, reconciling the world. In Jesus of Nazareth we have a visible, historical manifestation of God to whom we can express our love. There was nothing abstract about Jesus. He was a flesh-and-blood

person in whom God was uniquely present, the Word
made flesh dwelling among us in time and space. If we
need a mental image in order to think of God, let us
think of Jesus.

St. Bernard of Clairvaux, a twelfth-century French
monk, believed that God came to us in Jesus Christ in
order that we might have a visible object for our love. In
his twentieth sermon on the Song of Solomon, Bernard
wrote, "I think this is the principal reason why the
invisible God willed to be seen in the flesh and to
converse with men as man. He wanted to recapture the
affections of carnal men who were unable to love in any
other way, by first drawing them to the salutary love of
his own humanity, and then gradually to raise them to
a spiritual love."

If we have trouble loving God whom we cannot see,
we can love him in Jesus Christ who was God present in
history. So we meditate on the life of Jesus as a means
of deepening our knowledge of God.

There are many ways to meditate on the life of
Christ, but one of the classical methods was developed
in the sixteenth century by a Spaniard named Ignatius
of Loyola. It is explained in a book he wrote called *The
Spiritual Exercises*. Ignatius had prepared for a military career, but in one of his first battles he was severely
wounded and was forced to endure a long convales-
cence. Lacking anything else to do, he began to read
religious books and, as a result, was converted to a much
deeper understanding of Christian faith. He went on a
lengthy private retreat where he developed his meditative method, and later his work led to the founding of a
missionary group known as the Society of Jesus.

The Spiritual Exercises is a book designed to be used
on a four-week retreat. The aim of the system described
in it is to cause people to make important decisions

about their lives and to enable them to achieve a deeper union with God. For our purposes here, the directions for meditating on the life of Jesus might be helpful. The system requires serious attention and, ideally, the whole procedure is designed to be followed with the guidance of a spiritual director in order to avoid obvious dangers. However, the basic methodology can be useful to us in understanding the meditative possibilities in scripture.

Ignatius proposed that we take a passage from one of the Gospels describing an incident in the life of Jesus and apply his method to it. Throughout *The Spiritual Exercises* there are various instructions for meditation. What will be presented here is a composite of the various meditations he outlined. For our example, let us use Mark 1:16–20, the story of the call of four disciples.

There are four main parts in an Ignatian meditation:

> Preparatory Prayer
> Preludes
> Points for Meditation
> Colloquy and Lord's Prayer

The preparatory prayer is a request to God that all of our intentions, actions, and works may praise God. Every meditation should begin with this.

The preludes serve to put us in the proper frame of mind for the meditation. We cannot rush into a meditation very successfully. We must prepare ourselves by bringing our thoughts under control and opening our minds to be receptive to whatever may come to us. Ignatius prescribed three things for us to do in the preludes:

1. Think about the subject of the passage. What is this story about?

2. Develop a mental image of the place where the
incident occurred.
3. Ask what we desire from God.

The subject of our passage from Mark 1 is Jesus'
calling disciples. Jesus called people to follow him in
first-century Galilee, and he calls us to follow him
today. Our response to that call gives us much to
ponder.

As we begin to develop a mental image of the setting
of the story we think about Jesus walking along the
shore of the Sea of Galilee. We imagine a seacoast with
boats pulled up on the shore, fishnets hung out to dry,
the smell of the sea, birds in the air, the warm Palestin-
ian sun, perhaps a rocky coast.

Now we are to ask for what we desire. A clearer
awareness of God? The ability to respond to Christ's
call? More faithful discipleship on our part? A fruitful
meditation? The possibilities are limitless; it is a question of what we need in our lives right now.

Having prepared ourselves through these exercises,
we are now ready for the points for meditation.

Ignatius suggests three items to ponder:

1. Who is involved in this story?
2. What are they saying to each other?
3. What are they doing?

First, we are aware that there are many characters
in this story. Jesus, of course, is there. Simon, Andrew,
James, and John are the men called to be disciples. The
passage also mentions the presence of Zebedee, the
father of James and John, as well as some hired servants. Without doing violence to the passage we can
imagine the possibility of others who might be present:
other fishermen and workers, wives buying fish, chil-

dren playing up and down the coast. Perhaps there is a tax collector, maybe even some Roman soldiers patrolling. It could have been a busy place with a lot of activity.

Second, the dialogue taking place can be easily imagined. Jesus calls four people to follow him. Perhaps they discuss among themselves what this might mean. Maybe Zebedee offers some resistance, wondering who will help him in his fishing business if his sons leave. Other people, observing the scene, might comment to each other about Jesus and why these men are leaving their father. Perhaps the hired servants see more work ahead for themselves. There are many possibilities when thinking about what each person might have said. We might also give some thought to what it means to "fish for people."

The third point is the action taking place. What are people doing? They are fishing, they are mending nets, they are leaving their boats to follow Jesus. Children may be playing, adults may be gossiping, people may be buying and selling fish.

The point is that Ignatius wants us to look at the passage from as many angles as possible and put ourselves into the scene.

The last part of the Ignatian method involves a colloquy, a conversation with God. We might talk with God about our own response to the call to discipleship. We might ask for a deeper faith, one that would enable us to respond as the disciples did. We might ask what it really means to follow Christ, and we might also confess our hesitation. There are limits to our discipleship beyond which, for a variety of reasons, we are reluctant to go.

One of the major benefits of this system of meditation is that it gives us a sense of personal involvement in the events of Jesus' life. We are integrated into the sacred history through our meditation. It will be surprising to see how many new ideas come to us out of this kind of meditation if it is done with some regularity. We must remember, however, that this Jesus on whose life we meditate is not just a figure in the past. He is our contemporary; he is present now, in this moment in our lives. One of the great values of this system is that by putting ourselves in the presence of Christ through meditation, he becomes real to us, and we begin to discern his presence in our own existence.

The Ignatian method is a very precisely outlined meditative form. Although many of us would find it too rigid and artificial, it does force us to consider many aspects of a biblical passage. There is always the danger of letting our imagination run beyond the bounds of the text and sound theology, and we must guard against this. In fact, this is one of the reasons for working with a spiritual director. But this kind of meditation, if it is well disciplined, can profit us greatly in carefully examining the biblical presentation of the gospel.

The most important element in it, for the beginner, is that the system forces us to discipline our minds to meditate deeply. It ensures that our meditation will be carefully directed and will progress systematically. If some parts of the method do not work for us, we can discard them. Once we become reasonably proficient in meditation we can drop the rigid outline.

There are, of course, other parts of the Bible that are useful for meditation. Stories about Old Testament personalities and the life of Paul lend themselves to Ignatian-style meditation. This system can only be used with passages where there is a story being told. A mere list of teachings, such as the Sermon on the Mount or the epistle material, does not lend itself to this system.

There are, however, many rich passages worthy of pondering over and over in a more abstract manner: the Lord's Prayer in Matthew 6, the songs of Mary and Zechariah in Luke 1, Jesus' prayer for unity among his followers in John 17, and Paul's canticle praising the name of Jesus in Philippians 2.

Ultimately, of course, our goal in meditation is to probe more deeply the presence and reality of God. Since all mental images and conceptions of God are at best inadequate, we must strive to transcend them and become lost in the mystery of God. Spiritual writers call this experience "contemplation." It is a gift of God, the richest fruit of the spiritual life. It is indescribable. We cannot obtain it purely by our own effort, but we can develop our spirituality to the end that we are open and receptive to whatever God may give us. We can, by discipline and intention, grow in our experience of spiritual reality. One important step in this process is to diminish the ego, the "I." The more we focus on God, the less we tend to focus on ourselves. Meditation on scripture will help us set our sights on the transcendent and ultimate realities.

Prayer

4

Incline your ear, O LORD, and answer
 me,
 for I am poor and needy.
Preserve my life, for I am devoted to
 you;
 save your servant who trusts in
 you.
You are my God; be gracious to me, O
 Lord,
 for to you do I cry all day long.

Psalm 86:1–3

The psalmist expressed in this passage the feelings of every serious religious person. We sense our own spiritual poverty. We do not possess God. We have a desire for godliness, but perfection seems to lie just beyond our reach. Somehow, we know that we can be what we ought to be only through the gift of God's grace. So, we cry to God day and night for help. We long for the knowledge that God is with us. We pray.

Prayer takes many forms, ranging from the beauty and eloquence of traditional liturgical prayers to the nonverbal, unuttered desire for a closeness to God. It can sometimes be very frustrating; we pray and nothing happens. At other times it opens up the depths of our own selfhood. Like the other practices discussed in this book, prayer is of the greatest value when it is well disciplined. While anyone can pray anytime under any circumstances, a well ordered practice of prayer produces a much richer devotional life and increases the possibility of a deeper and clearer perception of God.

Prayer has been defined in many ways. Some writers have seen it as the ascent of the mind to God. Certainly it is an activity when our attention is focused directly on God. Others have described prayer as a dialogue in which we respond to the word and work of God. Prayer is our reaction to the revelation of what God is and what God has done. In view of the teachings of Jesus that God knows what we need before we ask, we might wonder if there is any point in praying at all. Even in this context, prayer is a way of acknowledging our total dependence upon God and the insufficiency of our own efforts. God does not need our prayers; we need our prayers. If we pray at all it is because we have hope in a transcendent Power that prevails over all of the forces of life.

The Bible admonishes us to pray. "Then Jesus told them a parable about their need to pray always and not to lose heart" (Luke 18:1). "Devote yourselves to prayer, keeping alert in it with thanksgiving" (Colossians 4:2). "Pray without ceasing" (1 Thessalonians 5:17). We are instructed to pray the Lord's Prayer (Matthew 6:9). But prayer is not just a duty and obligation; it is a source of joy. In John 16:24 Jesus said, "Until now you have not asked for anything in my name. Ask and you will receive, so that your joy may be complete."

Prayer was described by Paul as a gift from God. "We do not know how to pray as we ought, but that very Spirit intercedes with sighs too deep for words"

(Romans 8:26). The gospel is the proclamation that the grace of God covers our sins. That same grace covers our inability to pray. Even the desire to pray is a gift from God. Had God not been revealed to us in some way we would not even consider praying. We pray in response to God's self-disclosure and in the hope that God will act toward us in a loving manner. But most of all, we pray because of the stirring of the Holy Spirit within us.

While prayer is a benefit God gives us, it is sometimes a terrible problem for people. Yet, making it a problem is often just an excuse for not praying. There is really only one way to learn to pray and that is to pray. It is much easier to talk about prayer than to pull ourselves aside and get on with it.

The kind of praying that we do is a major factor in the kind of spiritual progress we make. If our prayer is undisciplined, irregular, and generally sloppy, prayer is going to mean very little to us. On the other hand, if it becomes an integral part of our living, if we do it on a regular basis whether we feel like it or not, and if it is well ordered, prayer will produce genuine spiritual growth.

In prayer we learn a great deal about ourselves. In fact, seeing ourselves as creatures of God, totally dependent upon divine mercy and power, is an essential insight for spiritual development. Our self-understanding and our experience of God are inseparably connected. The late Thomas Merton, one of the most popular spiritual writers of the twentieth century, said that our search for God cannot be fulfilled until we discover and enter into the deepest center of ourselves and understand our own helplessness. When we pray to God and the result is only emptiness and void, we begin to see very clearly that finding God by our own effort is no simple matter. We are struck by the harshness of our spiritual poverty. The realizations that we do not know God and that finding God is not as easy as we might have thought begin to create within us an openness that might enable us to perceive God's presence in our lives.

To use an ancient image in Christian spirituality, we must go into the desert before we can pray effectively. In the Bible, the desert seemed to have a purifying effect on people. The disobedient Israelites had to wander in the desert of Sinai until the first generation had passed away before they could enter the land God had promised them. Before Jesus began his ministry he spent forty days in the desert where he overcame temptation. Christian monasticism had its beginning when people began to leave the cities of North Africa where they felt the Christian life was impossible and fled to the desert to live alone with God.

In the desert is solitude, and in solitude we realize more clearly than otherwise our status before God. If we consider deeply the nature of prayer, we realize that we are seeking to establish communion with our Maker and our Judge who knows us better than we know ourselves, who is not deceived by our defense mechanisms, and who sees us as we really are. This can be a frightening position. When we stand alone before God, most of the things that we feel are important in life fade away and lose their significance. Our wealth, our fame, our prestige, our status, all mean nothing when we are alone with God. We are stripped of everything. We stand before God in absolute poverty. We experience our own nothingness, helplessness, and dependence. Almost all the things we have devoted most of our energy to acquire are valueless as far as our relationship with God is concerned. When we realize this, we understand the deepest meaning of poverty.

So, when we first begin seriously to pray, we recognize how far removed from God our lives are. It is terrifying to look into our hearts and minds and find chaos and confusion. We may go into interior solitude to find God and find absolutely nothing. It would probably be unusual if this were not our first reaction. This emptiness, this utter desolation, this experience of a spiritual desert, will help us to see that the God we claim to worship is really a stranger to us. John of the Cross called this the dark night of the soul. Painful though it may be, this experience is one of the prerequisites of spiritual development. Only when we are deeply aware of our real nature and spiritual condition are we ready to begin our spiritual quest. We simply cannot make spiritual progress if we are blocked by pride, if we think we know all there is to know about God, or if we are convinced of our own saintliness. Progress comes from the recognition of our poverty and emptiness. When we are overwhelmed by the mystery of God, then we are ready to begin probing that mystery and reflecting on those glimpses of God's presence that we are given. Then our prayer may gradually begin to increase our awareness of the reality of God in our lives and in the world.

It is sometimes said that the purpose of prayer is to bring God and people into communion with each other. But this is not achieved just by following the right techniques of prayer. What we can do, however, is to develop an openness in prayer that will make us more aware of the working of God within us. Prayer can help us remove the obstacles that blur our vision of God.

How do we begin? Where do we start in developing a serious effort at prayer? First, we must find some solitude. In modern society this is no easy task. As has already been mentioned, busy family schedules often make it difficult to find solitude in our homes. Certainly a blaring television or stereo can distract us from prayer as do the other noises of our environment. Perhaps a corner of the backyard, a walk around the block in the evening, a park, or an empty church can provide us with a quiet environment. Or, there may be times when we will stay up later or arise earlier than the rest of the family in order to have quiet time. In most cases, if we want it badly enough, we can find it. Certainly, we should guard against using the lack of quiet as an excuse. Excuses do not contribute anything to spiritual development.

Whether it is possible or not to find physical quiet, we must learn to develop an interior solitude by which we are able to shut out, at least temporarily, the noise and distractions around us. Sometimes we have to focus inwardly and ignore the things outside. In fact, in his book, *New Seeds of Contemplation*, Thomas Merton wrote, "There is no true solitude except interior solitude."

According to the Gospels, Jesus often sought solitude. He went into the wilderness; he drew apart from his disciples when he wanted to pray. He was alone in the garden at Gethsemane while some of the disciples slept. He admonished people to pray in secret. "Whenever you pray, go into your room and shut the door and pray to your Father who is in secret; and your Father who sees in secret will reward you" (Matthew 6:6). Whatever communion occurs between God and people often occurs in secret. There is no point in making a public performance of your prayer. People will not really be able to see what is taking place. Whatever intimacy develops with God will happen in secret.

Jesus warned his hearers against hypocrisy. Praying on the street corner in order to be seen defeats the purpose of prayer. Why should we try to deceive others with our prayer when God knows what we are really up to? Moreover, we can be ourselves more authentically when we are in solitude. We no longer have to worry about a public image. We can let down our guard, knowing that whatever happens is only between God and ourselves. In solitude we find the most freedom.

It is not always possible or even desirable for us suddenly to drop everything and pray. If prayer is to be done seriously, we must prepare ourselves for it. Ignatius of Loyola suggested that we stand a few feet from the place where we will actually pray and think about what we are going to do for a few minutes. We don't need to be that formal about it, but we should take time to make ourselves aware that we are about to confront the Divine Majesty.

Physical preparation is important. Whenever possible we must find the right physical environment: quiet, comfortable, free of distraction. Even physical posture is significant. Whether we stand, kneel, or sit does not really matter, but it is important that we find a happy medium between comfort and discomfort. We should not be tense or in pain, yet neither should we be so comfortable that we become drowsy or listless. Here a little self-denial can be a good thing. Whatever keeps us alert will be helpful. A hard chair might be better than a soft one. A slouchy, lazy posture will probably produce slouchy, lazy prayer.

What do we pray? What do we say to God? Do we merely unload problems about which God already knows? We find solitude and quiet; what do we do with it? If we are unable to formulate prayers in our minds, we could do well by praying the Psalms. As we have already seen, they express our deepest religious feelings, and there are few prayers that we could pray

better than these. We can become familiar enough with
the Psalms that they become our own prayers because
they express the basic religious desires of everyone.

There is another method of prayer that might be of
some help to the beginner. It comes from Eastern
Orthodox Christianity and is very ancient, dating back
at least until the fifth century, perhaps earlier. It
involves the use of what is variously called the Jesus
Prayer or the Prayer of the Heart. Previously mentioned in Chapter 2, the prayer is simple: "Lord Jesus
Christ, Son of God, have mercy on me a sinner."

It is a very complete prayer, containing everything
we need. It acknowledges our spiritual poverty: We are
sinners. It expresses our need for divine mercy. That is
our greatest need in life. Most important of all, it affirms
the lordship of Jesus Christ who brought us the gospel
of God's mercy.

The prayer has several biblical roots. The most
obvious is the parable of the Pharisee and the tax
collector in Luke 18. Both men went up to the temple to
pray. The Pharisee offered a self-righteous prayer thank-
ing God that he was not like other people who did not
tithe or fast and who lived immorally. The tax collector
beat his breast, looked to heaven, and prayed, "God, be
merciful to me, a sinner!"

The prayer was also based on the belief that there
was spiritual power in pronouncing the name of Jesus.
In his marvelous Christological hymn in Philippians 2,
Paul described the name of Jesus as one "that is above
every name" at the hearing of which "every knee should
bend, in heaven and on earth and under the earth, and
every tongue should confess that Jesus Christ is Lord."
While this may sound a bit strange to Western Protestant ears, notice how many of our popular hymns are
based on the name of Jesus: "All Hail the Power of Jesus'

Name," "Jesus, the Very Thought of Thee," "Jesus, Thou Joy of Loving Hearts," "How Sweet the Name of Jesus Sounds." We have sung a chorus, "Jesus, Jesus, Jesus, sweetest name I know. Fills my every longing, keeps me singing as I go."

Eastern Orthodox Christians developed a tradition of repeating this prayer constantly throughout the day. They believed that such prayer would generate mystical union with God. Some people developed certain physical postures to be used while reciting the prayer in time with their breathing. The prayer was often adjusted to "Lord Jesus Christ, have mercy on me," or simply "Christ have mercy."

This simple one sentence prayer has produced a substantial amount of literature. The *Philokalia* is a collection of essays on the Jesus Prayer written between the fourth and fifteenth centuries by Orthodox writers. It was compiled by two Greek monks and first published in 1782.

A more popular book, *The Way of the Pilgrim*, has made Westerners aware of the Jesus Prayer in modern times. The book appeared in Russia in the nineteenth century and is of anonymous authorship. It describes the travels and adventures of a Russian peasant and his experiences with the Jesus Prayer. He entered a church one day and heard the priest read 1 Thessalonians 5:17, "Pray without ceasing." He wondered how it would be possible for anyone to do this. He eventually encountered a Russian starets or spiritual teacher who taught him the Jesus Prayer. Under the guidance of this man the peasant worked his way up to praying the Jesus Prayer twelve thousand times a day. Eventually he found that he did not have to make a conscious effort to pray it, but the prayer simply prayed itself in his heart so that he was, in fact, praying without ceasing. The rest of the book describes his experiences with other people and his own religious development that resulted from the use of the prayer. At one point the peasant said, "I roamed about through many different places for a long time with the Prayer of Jesus as my sole companion. It gladdened and comforted me in all my wanderings, my meetings with other people and in all the incidents of the journey."

More recently, the prayer has been dealt with in a little novel by J. D. Salinger called *Franny and Zooey*. Franny was a student in a New England college who was introduced to the Jesus Prayer in a religion class. In the first part of the novel she tries rather unsuccessfully to explain to her boyfriend the use of the Jesus Prayer by telling him about *The Way of the Pilgrim*. When her skeptical friend asks what the purpose of it is, she says, "You get to see God. Something happens in some absolutely nonphysical part of the heart—where the Hindus say the Atman resides, if you ever took any Religion—and you see God, that's all."

We might regard these claims as too extravagant, and this kind of devotional procedure probably suited the Eastern mind better than it does ours. But the use of the prayer has been a part of Orthodox devotional tradition for centuries. We could use it as a means of beginning our prayer, repeating it as often as we wish or feel necessary. After all, the basic prayer of any Christian is a prayer for the mercy of God. Although there may be many things we want, that is what we need the most. If nothing else, the prayer might be useful in settling us down and putting us in a proper frame of mind for prayer. We could use it before church on Sunday morning as we wait for the service to begin, during the serving of communion, or in any short period of silence that might suddenly become available. The

New Testament instructs us to pray in the name of Jesus, and this simple prayer makes a good beginning for us.

The greatest of all the traditional prayers, of course, is the Lord's Prayer. Whenever we are at a loss for words to pray, we can pray this prayer. It contains all the elements of good prayer: praise, an affirmation that the will of God is best for people, a request for daily bread, and a plea for forgiveness and protection from evil. What more do we really need? In a brief treatise called *A Simple Way to Pray*, Martin Luther wrote, "To this day I suckle at the Lord's Prayer like a child, and as an old man eat and drink from it and never get my fill. It is the very best prayer, even better than the psalter, which is so very dear to me. It is surely evident that a real master composed and taught it."

Luther suggested building our prayers around each phrase in the Lord's Prayer. At one particular time we might concentrate on the words "Hallowed be Thy name." At another we might consider a different phrase, such as, "Forgive us our trespasses as we forgive those who trespass against us." The prayer is a rich treasure house of material for personal prayer and meditation.

Eventually, we will want to move beyond the repetition of traditional prayers, although they are always useful. There are basically three types of prayer that we need to consider: praise, confession, and petition. People whose prayer life is undisciplined and irregular will probably concentrate on the third, but all three are essential for a balanced devotional life.

Praise may well be the most difficult type of prayer because we are trying to praise a God we do not know very well. At least we can praise God for certain actions: the creation of the world, the gift of life, the love shown in Jesus Christ. As our understanding and experience of

God deepen, we will praise God for the divine action in our own personal lives. But even this is an inferior form of praise. St. Bernard, in his little book, *On Loving God*, said that the only reason for loving God is God. The deeper we probe into the mystery of God, the more we can praise simply because God is God. Thanksgiving is an important part of our praise, but we must move beyond even that and praise God because we have become lost in the mystery of Divinity.

Bernard also answered the question of how much we should love God by saying that we should love beyond measure. Our love for God should not be based only on what God has done for us, but should be a love of that ineffable mystery to which we give ourselves without reservation. It is this kind of love that makes it possible for us to praise God in good times and in bad, when things go well for us and when we face senseless misery and tragedy.

Our ability to praise God is directly related to our spiritual development. If our understanding of God is simplistic and rigid, our ability to praise will be very limited. If we are convinced that we have the final word of truth about God, our praise will be restricted by our conception of God. If, however, we sense that God is far greater than our capacity to understand, that God transcends our intellectual abilities, and that we are overwhelmed by a power about which we will never know more than just the tiniest bit, praise will come easy and will be a natural response. We praise God, not because God needs our praise, but because we are compelled to respond. What may have been difficult at the beginning of our spiritual life may ultimately become the only kind of prayer we pray. We may not understand all there is to life, but we can praise God who is sovereign over all things.

The second type of praise is prayer of confession. This can be a painful experience, but in many ways a cleansing and refreshing one. God knows our faults better than we do. The point of this kind of prayer is that we acknowledge our failures and affirm that God can overcome them. The worst thing about our sins is that they are offenses against God. Many of the people to whom we do evil may well eventually recover from it. Life is going to go on. It is bad enough that we do evil that disrupts the lives of others, but more serious than that is our violation of our commitment to discipleship. We violate our baptism. We reject, at least temporarily, what we believe to be the will of God for us. In the instance in which we do evil, we reject God and presume to know more than God does about what is good for us. So our primary offense is against God. More than anything else, sin is a lack of faith and trust that the will and purposes of God are right for us.

Beyond that, there is something about our human nature that seems to incline us toward selfishness. A force deep within us tries to pull us back from our search for God. For Paul, sin is not just an immoral act. It is a defect in our character, our nature, that keeps us from being what we know we should be as Christian people and tends to push us toward destructive behavior. That is why we have wars and injustice and other evils in the world, and why peace between and among people seems so elusive. The apostle expressed it clearly in Romans 7: "I do not understand my own actions. For I do not do what I want, but I do the very thing I hate. Now if I do what I do not want...it is no longer I that do it, but sin that dwells within me....I can will what is right, but I cannot do it. For I do not do the good I want, but the evil I do not want is what I do. Now if I do what I do not want, it is no longer I that do it, but sin that dwells within me.

So I find it to be a law that when I want to do what is good, evil lies close at hand. For I delight in the law of God in my inmost self, but I see in my members another law at war with the law of my mind, making me captive to the law of sin that dwells in my members. Wretched man that I am! Who will rescue me from this body of death? Thanks be to God through Jesus Christ our Lord!"

So we confess our sin, however, in confidence that God will forgive us according to the promises of the gospel. In 1 John 1:8–9 we find a summary of the gospel: "If we say that we have no sin, we deceive ourselves, and the truth is not in us. If we confess our sins, he who is faithful and just will forgive us our sins and cleanse us from all unrighteousness."

One of the traditional spiritual exercises in Christianity is the examination of conscience. This must be done before an adequate prayer of confession can be prayed. Ignatius of Loyola, whose meditative methods were discussed in Chapter 3, developed a procedure that he called "General Examination of Conscience." There are five steps to follow:

1. We give thanks for what God has done for us.
2. We ask for the grace to know our sins and free ourselves from them.
3. We examine what we have done during the day. First we examine our thoughts, then what we have said, and, finally, our actions.
4. We ask God's forgiveness for our failures.
5. We resolve to change our lives. The exercise is closed with the Lord's Prayer.

A regular examination of conscience is a good practice. Doing it on a daily basis is not always easy, but doing it too infrequently will defeat the purpose, which is to make us aware of our human nature, our need for God's grace, and the vigilance required to deal with evil.

A warning should be injected here. While regular examination of conscience is of great value, we must not fall into a constant brooding about how bad we are. Harboring guilt feelings can create serious problems for us. The good news of the gospel is that God has forgiven us. "We have an advocate with the Father, Jesus Christ the righteous; and he is the atoning sacrifice for our sins, and not for ours only but also for the sins of the whole world" (1 John 2:1–2). Let us be honest with ourselves, repentant for the evil we have done. But then let us turn this over to God in the hope of forgiveness and the promise of new life in Jesus Christ. What has been done is done, and it will be taken care of by God's love and grace. We should seek to begin anew looking ahead and let the past take care of itself. Opportunities for living our faith are before us; let us not be held back by the guilt of the past.

If we need help in evaluating our lives we might return to the Bible for guidance. For example, we might use the Ten Commandments as a measuring rod. How does each of them apply to us? Have we had any other gods before us? Have we regarded anything else as more important than God? Have we taken God's name in vain? Have we stolen anything? Did we cheat on taxes or a business transaction? Did we bear false witness? Did we lie? Did we tell hearsay gossip as if it were the certain truth? Have we coveted others' possessions? Have we ever felt that we would be happier if we were married to someone else, lived in a different place, or had someone else's job? Each of the Ten Commandments has broad application. Idolatry is more than just worshiping a golden calf and stealing is more than just taking an item from someone's home or store. We should think deeply on the broader significance of these moral teachings.

If we think we measure up pretty well on these points, we might turn to the Sermon on the Mount in Matthew 5—7 where Jesus made the commandments considerably more difficult. He said that it was not enough just to refrain from the act of adultery. Adultery can be committed in our hearts. It was not enough to refrain from killing; we must not be angry with another. We are told to love our enemies, avoid judgment, resist not one who is evil, and turn the other cheek. Here is an ethic that is virtually impossible to live. If taken seriously, the Sermon on the Mount will drive us to our knees in a plea for grace and forgiveness.

The third type of prayer is petition, asking God for something specific for ourselves or for others. Early in our spiritual development it may seem the most important and frequently used form of prayer. As we progress, however, it will become less important as we realize that what we want is to know the presence of God more than the things God can do for us.

However, it must be said that there is nothing wrong with a prayer of petition. Some people have told me that they feel guilty about asking God for anything. They do not want to be regarded as selfish. Of course, there are some requests that are not worthy of prayer. We should ask only for what is fitting. Still, it is a sign of spiritual growth when we can affirm that all we have ultimately comes from God and that our lives are lived under God's sovereignty. It is right to pray for world peace, for good health for those we love, for a deeper faith, for reconciliation among people, or for forgiveness. A major section of the Lord's Prayer is an appeal for daily bread.

The quality of our petitions will be determined by the depth of our spirituality. The closer we live to God, the more things we once thought we had to have will seem less important. Jesus did not restrict our petitions; he only insisted that we not pray hypocritically. In any event, God will receive our prayers. The gospel promise is that prayers are heard and responded to, although the response may not always be what we expect. The most important thing about prayer is not asking and receiving; it is acknowledging that we live in the presence of God and that we are dependent people. If we focus on God alone, we need feel no guilt about prayers of petition.

A short postscript should be added to this discussion of petition, however. We ought to be careful about what we pray for because our prayer might be answered. If we pray, for example, for the destruction of evil, we might find some things removed from our lives that we really did not want taken away. If we pray that the will of God be done, we might experience some radical changes in our lives. If we pray for a deeper faith, we might find our values changing more drastically than we had expected. There is always a certain risk in prayer, a risk that the answer might affect our lives in very important ways.

As our prayer life progresses we will probably experience a gradual change in our style of prayer. Christian mystics have often said that the deepest kind of prayer is nonverbal. The experience of those who have developed a strong devotional life is that early in the process prayer is verbal, there is some effort to make it eloquent, and it is carefully worded. In time, however, verbal prayer becomes simpler, eloquent language disappears, and only minimal wording is used. For example, a prayer such as, "Almighty God, who calls us to be peacemakers, send thy Spirit to the warring nations of the world that people might lay down their arms and be reconciled with each other as brothers and sisters," may simply become, "For peace in the world." The Lord's Prayer, certainly, is an example of simplicity and the use of minimal language.

In nonverbal prayer we use no words, no mental images, no concepts. Rather, our prayer is just a matter of feeling, of loving, of longing for God. Now we cannot find words that are adequate to express what we feel, we can only express ourselves with emotions. When words are no longer sufficient, when we recognize the poverty of language, we are making real progress.

Finally, a word must be said about the role of self-denial in prayer. In the history of Christianity asceticism has taken many forms. Medieval monks practiced fasting, self-flagellation, the wearing of hair shirts, and celibacy, among other things, as means of self-discipline. Protestantism has generally rejected such practices although many churches have encouraged temperance in the use of alcohol, tithing, the avoidance of extravagance, and similar practices as means of fulfilling Jesus' command that his followers deny themselves.

Self-denial for the sake of self-denial is of no value to the Christian. Self-denial practiced in order to orient our lives toward God alone becomes not a burden but a joy. As far as life in the spirit is concerned, the denial we must practice in these days involves the use of our time. Most of us can give up many things more easily than we can give up time. However, in order to develop a deep spiritual life we must take time normally used for other things and devote it to prayer. Making good use of time is a modern form of Christian asceticism.

The rhythm of our lives is often established by our work or job. We may let it be influenced by other things such as family needs, community involvement, or the daily television schedule. The control of time is a crucially important matter. Once gone, it can never be reclaimed. We must deny some of this time to other purposes and use it for our search for God. Like many things in life, prayer will not become an exhilarating and satisfying activity until we have practiced it to the point that we are proficient. Any beginning effort in athletics, the arts, even business, can be frustrating and discouraging until we have developed proficiency through experience. Self-denial is part of the training that leads to the kind of satisfaction that comes from doing something well.

Prayer is essential to the Christian life, for it is here that we have the most intimate relationship with God. Without it, our other activities will lack a certain depth of motivation and understanding. In one of his commentaries on the Bible, John Calvin, the reformer of Geneva, summarized the purpose of Christian prayer. "When we set out to pray," he wrote, "there are two things we must seek above all: first, that we may have access to God, and secondly, that we may rest in him with full and solid confidence, knowing his Fatherly love for us and his unbounded kindness."

Making Progress 5

Who shall ascend the hill of the LORD?
And who shall stand in his holy
place?
Those who have clean hands and pure
hearts,
who do not lift up their souls to
what is false.

Psalm 24:3–4

The ideas that have been explained so far represent only the first steps in a serious devotional life. Their purpose is to lead us to something deeper, and when we do not need these things anymore we should discard them and move on to something else. In attempting to develop spiritually, however, we must realize that we can always make more progress in exploring the mystery of God. Deeper insight and understanding are always possible. God is far too vast for us fully to understand. In fact, it is a miracle, a breaking into the human by the Divine, if we know anything about God at all. Once we take the attitude that we have gone as far

71

as we need to go, our spiritual life is dead. We must not stop at the beginning point. Any experience with the Divine or any understanding of God is always inadequate; our humanity will always get in the way. Spiritual development, then, is a lifelong process. There is always something new to discover and experience.

The spiritual life is not always sweetness and light. We will not experience steady, upward progress in our development. There will be bad times, times of discouragement, periods of deep frustration. We will be tempted to give it up and assume that it is not worth the effort or that there is really nothing to religion after all. It is important to know that such problems lie ahead of us and that we can cope with them.

As has already been mentioned, spiritual development is a journey through the desert. There will be few trees to shade us and few oases to quench our thirst. The presence of a desert will discourage some people from making the journey because the way is hard and the route uncertain. It is easy to get lost. Therefore, it is essential that we travel light. An experienced camper can always get along on less equipment than a beginner needs. In traveling through this desert we must leave behind a lot of useless baggage. This will include values that will not help us, preconceived notions that may be inadequate, and a love for things we cannot have. Fame, prestige, influence, power over others, luxury, and reputation will be of no use to us whatsoever in the desert. Unless we detach ourselves from a love for them, they will slow us down and hinder our progress.

God must be our guide in the desert. We may be reasonably certain that we know the route, but the desert plays tricks on us. The heat causes us to see mirages and the barren wasteland looks the same in any direction. If God does not direct us we will become hopelessly lost. We must trust God, like Israel on her journey to the promised land, or we will never get out of the desert. Faith is a precondition for spiritual development, and the faithfulness of God is the map that guides us.

We have already looked at some of the equipment we need for our journey: silence, meditation, and prayer. Beyond these we need some basic attitudes that require decision making on our part. These can best be described by looking at the teachings of some of the best known Christian mystics on the problems of spiritual progress.

Saint Bonaventure lived in the thirteenth century. He was a member of the Franciscan order and, for a time, a theological professor in Paris. Among his many writings on the spiritual life is a small book entitled *The Triple Way*. He believed that the contemplation of God was the highest attainment of life, and in this little book he explained the steps we must take to achieve that goal. The first is *purgation*. We must attempt to purge ourselves of evil and to strive for purity of heart. We must be truly sorry for the evil we have done, the evil in which we are caught socially and cannot control, and confess our sins to God. The second step is *illumination*. Here we should apply reason and intelligence to increasing our knowledge of God. We should consider the nature of God's mercy and forgiveness and the promises of the gospel. Hopefully, this leads to the third step, which is *union* with God. This comes from turning our attention away from the world of things and focusing on God alone, directing all of our love toward our Creator.

The route of spiritual progress for St. Bonaventure is clear: repentance, growth in understanding, intimacy with God. This has become a classical formulation in Christian spirituality and indicates that there is not

instant mystical experience or awareness of God. These
blessings are often the result of a long process of growth
and development.

St. Bernard, the twelfth-century Cistercian monk,
preached eighty-six sermons on the first two chapters of
the Song of Solomon. On the face of it, the Song of
Solomon is a poem about two lovers and their affection
for each other. Bernard, however, saw it as a treatise on
the spiritual life. The relationship between the bride
and the bridegroom, he said, was an allegory of the
relationship between Christ and the Christian.

The second verse of the book says, "Let him kiss me
with the kisses of his mouth." For Bernard, the kiss was
a useful image. Our spiritual development, he said, can
be explained in terms of three kisses. The first stage is
represented by the kiss of the feet. A medieval servant,
having offended the master, would beg forgiveness by
kissing the master's feet. This kind of kiss, for Bernard,
symbolized repentance. Spiritual development begins
by recognizing our need for God's mercy and asking for
forgiveness. The second kiss is the kiss of the hand. This
refers to Christ taking us by the hand and pulling us up
from whatever we might have been to newness of life.
This step requires that we amend our lives and grow in
virtue. Finally, the third step is the kiss of the mouth.
The intimacy of lovers is an allegory of our union with
God. This is the highest form of the kiss and represents
the summit of religious experience.

In these sermons Bernard made it clear that our
growth in the knowledge of God is directly related to our
growth in virtue. Moral and ethical improvement is a
prerequisite to spiritual growth. "Blessed are the pure
in heart, for they will see God" (Matthew 5:8). We
cannot expect to know God in the world if our relations
with the world are based on deception, falsehood, self-

ishness, cheating, and violence. How can we be open and honest with God if we are not the same with each other? Psalm 15 teaches us that the people who will sojourn in God's tent and dwell on God's holy hill are those who "walk blamelessly, and do what is right, and speak the truth from their heart; who do not slander with their tongue, and do no evil to their friends, nor take up a reproach against their neighbors" (Psalm 15:2–3). We cannot experience the reality of God on a very deep level until we have made some serious changes in our lives. Bernard warned his monks not to expect too much too soon. They should not expect the kind of experience with God for which they were not yet ready.

I once talked with a spiritual director in a religious community about this very point. This was a man of wide experience. A former chemical engineer, he held a Ph.D. in chemistry from a great Midwestern university and had worked for a major oil company for many years. Later he became a monk, went to seminary, and was ordained. "What," I asked him, "do you tell people when they say they cannot pray anymore?" He replied, "I ask them how they are living." When there is something wrong with our prayer life, there is probably something wrong with the way we are living that needs to be examined.

The writer of 1 John put it very directly: "Beloved, let us love one another, because love is from God; everyone who loves is born of God and knows God. Whoever does not love does not know God, for God is love" (1 John 4:7–8). We cannot hate and know God. We cannot live full of hostility and anger and know God. The same point was made in *The Cloud of Unknowing*, an anonymous spiritual classic written in fourteenth-century England. The author wrote, "By love may He be gotten and holden, but by thought never." To know God we must develop a lifestyle based on love. This is even more important than the development of devotional disciplines.

This means that the active and contemplative lives cannot be separated. Among many church people there is a tendency to classify Christians as either pietists or social activists. This is a false distinction. There can be no genuine Christian piety apart from a deep concern for people and their problems in the world. Likewise, social activism that is not grounded in a strong relationship with God will not get at the root problems of humanity.

This is why Christians must withdraw for brief periods of renewal and a deeper penetration into the mystery of God. Our perception of God will help us put our work in the world in its proper perspective.

One of the biggest problems in spiritual growth is the occurrence of the so-called "dry times" when nothing seems to happen. We read and cannot remember a single thing we read. We pray and all is emptiness. In silence we are restless and our minds will not settle down. God seems unreal and nothing we do brings any hope. It is, as John of the Cross called it, a dark night of the soul. It is being completely lost in the desert and not knowing which way to go. Such times can defeat us, and people who say they have never faced such dry times in their religious lives have probably not taken their spiritual development very seriously.

There are several things we can do to cope with this problem. The first and most important is to realize that it is going to happen. No matter how dedicated we are, how much faith we have, or how much we love God, it appears to be a part of the psychology of religious experience that the dry times will come. Read the writings of the great saints and you will see that they all struggled with the same problem.

If you should decide to begin a program of vigorous physical exercise, such as jogging, after having lived a sedentary existence for years, it will not be long before your body will cry out in rebellion. Your muscles will ache with pain, you may find it uncomfortable to walk or sit in certain positions, and sleep may be impossible. You will wonder if it is worth it and will be tempted to give up. Only gradually will your muscles begin to respond and your wind and endurance develop. You will also find that having achieved a certain level of physical conditioning you will have to continue exercising on a regular basis or you will lose all you have gained.

The spiritual life faces the same problems. Having ignored the spiritual side of life and depended solely on temporal things all our lives, no significant change of orientation can take place without painful struggle. It will be easy to lapse back into the old values and old ways of looking at the world. We may give up some old attitudes without knowing for sure what new attitudes to adopt. We may come to see that there is nothing of any permanent importance except God, but having not yet found God, we find ourselves living in a desert. We do not want to go back where we were, but we are not at all sure what lies ahead. A deep frustration may develop. Many Christian mystics have described periods of intense suffering as part of their spiritual growth.

The act of prayer may seem a quiet, restful act. In fact, however, deep prayer may require considerable energy and concentration because practically everything in our lives distracts us. Communion with God requires a reorientation toward so many things that press in upon our lives, and this cannot be done without a struggle. The temptation to give up will be ever present and, if we lack self-discipline or cannot break ourselves away from things that obscure our vision of God, the journey will be more difficult.

Even when we make significant progress the danger of regression is still with us. Because of our prayer and meditation we may sense the reality of God and know a deep peace. There may be occasions, especially when we are outside the normal routine of our lives, when we experience the presence of God in such a self-authenticating way that our whole view of life is radically altered. We may reach a level of spiritual growth where we know in ways we have never known before that God is indeed present and sovereign, and that life can be lived on the most abundant level when we are in communion with the Divine.

But in a relatively short time the experience passes, and there sets in a tendency to lapse back into old attitudes. It becomes more difficult to find time for devotional activity, and when we do steal a few moments for it the experience is dry and empty. It has been pointed out by many that the world wars of this century, the rise of Nazism and communism, and the impossibility of keeping peace, have demonstrated how easy it is for highly civilized people to fall back into barbarianism. Chaos is always seething just below the surface. But we must not allow ourselves to be defeated. Some hope can be taken in the fact that the dark night appears to be a common experience of people seriously engaged in spiritual development. We must not fear it. We should expect it and be ready for it. Most important of all, we must have faith that the grace of God will carry us through it.

A second way of dealing with the problem of aridity is to wait for God. Ultimately, spiritual progress is a grace. Whatever we experience of God happens because God lets it happen. Even the Spirit prays in us, said Paul. Part of our problem may be in attempting to push ourselves to a level for which we are not yet ready. If we are called to the spiritual life, our best attitude is one of waiting in emptiness in the expectation that God will do something. In short, the spiritual life demands of us faith, a faith that if this is what God wants us to do, God will provide us with what we need. If we have this faith we can wait without anxiety and fear, resting in the love of God.

People frequently ask whether they should try to pray or meditate during these dry times. In general, the answer is yes. We do not know what may be developing unconsciously within us. Maintaining a discipline over a long period of time will produce growth even if some days seem to be unproductive. What is important is not one prayer or one day or week, but the totality of our devotional experience.

We can always profit from praying the Psalms. The Bible is filled with prayers that we might use when we can formulate none of our own. We can still explore the depths of silence. At the very least, we can go through the devotional procedures we have established for ourselves. A day should be sanctified by prayer, even if it is a bad day.

It may be that some of the devotional practices we use do not serve us well and should be dropped or forgotten. However, we must not use this as an excuse for doing nothing or neglecting the spiritual life. It would seem prudent always to pray, in good times and in bad. We never know what the cumulative effect of daily prayer might be.

A third thing we can do is to work with a spiritual director. It is very important, in view of all the dangers and pitfalls of the spiritual life, that we seek the guidance of someone who is competent, who has a deep devotional life of his or her own, and whom we can trust. Such people are not easy to find. The church demands so much administrative work of its clergy that ministers have difficulty finding time for spiritual direction. This is an area where the whole attitude of the institutional church needs reform and renewal.

Still, there are people around who take the spiritual life seriously, and can give us guidance. Church sponsored programs on prayer and spiritual life retreats will often introduce us to knowledgeable people. If all else fails, we can do some serious spiritual reading. The Christian tradition has a rich treasury of literature on spirituality. The best of these writers exhibit a timeless quality in their writings, for spiritual problems are fundamentally the same in every age. Some will speak to us more helpfully than others, but reading of the experiences of those who have developed a deep spiritual life can be a fine source of guidance.

The works of the great theologians of the church can also help us. They can give fresh insights into the nature of God and the meaning of Jesus Christ. But more than this, the best of them will make us aware of the vastness of the mystery of God, a mystery that, if recognized, will overwhelm us. If we engage in devotional activity because we want to find answers to specific questions or want to have certain kinds of "experiences" we will be frustrated. The ultimate goal of the spiritual life is to immerse ourselves in the mystery of God, a mystery that transcends all conceptualizing, reason, or sense experience. When we are surrounded and overwhelmed by the mystery of God, the questions and the experiences fade into insignificance. God alone is enough. Therefore, in our devotional lives we must take what

God gives us, give thanks for it, and not insist on having everything go the way we want it.

Two points here need elaboration. The first is the place of reason in religious experience. The spiritual life is not hostile to reason and certainly is not anti-intellectual. Many Christian mystics have been intellectuals in the fullest and best sense of the word. Christian spirituality is appreciative of anything that reason or intellectual activity can teach us about God. But it does understand that God far transcends our ability to understand or explain fully the Divine with the normal intellectual tools. The usefulness of reason has limits. In the deepest kind of prayer there is only a profound awareness of God that cannot be explained intelligibly or described with concepts.

The other point is that we cannot let our spiritual development depend upon any particular kind of experiences. The word *experience* has been used a good bit in this book, but it has been intended to mean any awareness of God that we might have. It does not mean visions, miracles, feeling a warm glow inside, or ecstatic utterances. These things may occur and have had their place in the history of Christian spirituality, but what we are seeking in the spiritual life is not an experience, but God.

Many people think they are making no progress in the spiritual life unless they are sustained by a series of emotional experiences. The danger with this, of course, is that they begin to seek the experience rather than God. And, when the experience is over they tend to think they have nothing. We must learn to be indifferent to highly emotional experiences. To live on them in the spiritual life is like living on drugs in the world. What we seek is a clean, clear perception of the presence of God at work in our lives.

I have worked with many college students on retreats and in meetings where they have had experiences that they felt would change their lives forever. Yet, a few months later the glow had faded, the experience was forgotten, and life was back to normal. It takes something much deeper than this to sustain spiritual growth. If all we want is an experience, we really don't have to look very far. Enough is known about mass psychology today to manipulate the environment in such a way that an emotional experience is produced. Actors and entertainers know how to do it, and so do some professional evangelists. But a contrived religious experience is not our goal; our goal is an awareness of God.

There is always a tendency to regress or backslide in our religious development. This is faced day by day in a disciplined life of prayer, not every six months with an emotional experience.

What, then, are the signs of progress in the spiritual life? A major one is the development of an appreciation for quiet and solitude to the point that we no longer have to push and drive ourselves to pray, meditate, and read. There will always be temptations to stop these practices, but in general, the more we taste and see, the more we will welcome those times when we can engage in deep contemplative activity. Such practices will cease being things to do and evaluate and will become more natural parts of our living.

Another development will probably be a tendency toward less verbalizing in prayer and less conceptualizing of divine things. We will feel less of a need for words and images, although we will never completely discard them. One of the characteristics of a deep perception of God is that it cannot be communicated to someone else. We lack adequate vocabulary and imagery for such descriptions.

A greater willingness to trust God is another obvious fruit of the spiritual life. The more we sense the Divine, the less we feel that we have to depend upon things. This, of course, produces a deeper peace as we grow in the realization that everything ultimately depends upon God and that God's love is sovereign over all opposition.

The greatest manifestation of spiritual growth is a deepening love for both God and the human family. If we have made significant progress, we will be more open to God's self-revelation and more open to other people who we realize are created in the image of God. The more we know God the more we will love God, and the more love we have the less we will allow hatred and jealousy and envy to weaken our character. This is the work of love within us.

Moreover, a genuine love for God and other people will deepen our social concern. It is impossible to love and be tolerant of suffering, hunger, injustice, want, and oppression. A spirituality that does not produce a stronger social concern is a false spirituality. We cannot love God and be indifferent to God's children. In this sense, an authentic spiritual life generates some agony as we increasingly identify with the miseries of suffering humanity.

The summit of the spiritual life, never fully reached in this life, is the contemplation of God. As used in Christian spiritual classics, contemplation has two levels of meaning. Acquired contemplation involves whatever experience of God we can have as a result of our own efforts. The higher level of contemplation, however, is infused contemplation. This is a gift of grace, an awareness of the divine that God has given us. This kind of contemplation cannot be produced by our own efforts, but in it God overcomes our human limitations and grants us a perception of reality that is clear and alive. It is an awakening to God, an enlightening, an insight that God is. It is a realization that our own true selfhood is found only in God.

Devotional Procedures 6

Seven times a day I praise you
for your righteous ordinances.

Psalm 119:164

Somewhere in a book like this we must deal with practicalities. What are the specific things we do to develop ourselves spiritually? We have discussed in general terms various techniques: prayer, meditation, the use of silence, and reading. How do we fit these into our daily lives?

A contemplative attitude toward life is far more important than any set of procedures we might follow. There is a sense in which the spiritual life is more of an attitude, an orientation toward life, than anything else. I once heard of a Buddhist monastery in Vietnam where young monks were not allowed to meditate until they first learned to open doors and serve tea and perform other very ordinary duties as contemplative acts. Contemplatives have a way of seeing great value and significance in the simplest, most commonplace activities of life. It is important to do simple things well. When we can do common tasks as contemplative acts, we are well along in our spiritual development. It is foolish to expect any kind of deep spiritual progress when little things irritate us or when we are always venting our rage about things that do not go right for us. If we are abrasively aggressive, prone to lose our tempers, and always trying to force our will on other people, we will find quiet devotional activity virtually impossible.

In its classical, monastic form, the contemplative life has been composed of three basic elements: prayer, work, and reading. The goal has been to maintain a careful balance among these elements. None can be ignored and none can be overemphasized at the expense of others. Work is essential for most people. The only question is whether we can approach it with a sense of vocation or out of simple economic necessity. Prayer must be done on some kind of regular and disciplined basis. Reading is of great importance, for here we encounter new ideas that stretch our minds, clarify faith, and produce growth.

It is important that we set a daily routine for prayer and meditation. Speaking in one of his sermons of the "utter darkness" in some people's lives, John Wesley said, "Perhaps no sin of omission more frequently occasions this than the neglect of private prayer; the want whereof cannot be supplied by any other ordinance whatever." Elsewhere Wesley wrote, "We have need daily to retire from the world, at least morning and evening, to converse with God, to commune more freely with our Father who is in secret." Martin Luther described his own procedure when his faith began to cool: "I take my little psalter, hurry to my room...and, as time permits, I say quietly to myself and word for word the Ten Commandments, the Creed, and, if I have time, some words of Christ or of Paul, or some psalms, just as a child might do."

The possibilities for devotional activity are many. What works for someone else might not work for us, but we must establish some regular procedure if we want to grow spiritually. If we pray only when we feel like it, we probably won't pray very much. Contemplatives have always found a need for self-denial. Giving up part of our time is something everyone can afford, but it often requires a firm resolve and deep commitment when so many other demands are pressing in upon us.

The content and length of a daily devotional routine will vary for each individual and his or her circumstances. However, there are a few general principles that are applicable to almost everyone. Whatever we do must be done regularly. Occasional spurts of activity followed by inactivity because we are too busy are rather useless. However, we should not feel great guilt when something makes it impossible for us to follow our routine on a given day. Our purpose is not to maintain a routine; our purpose is to find God. Nevertheless, we must be able to pray with regularity through the ups and downs, the good times and the bad times of life. We need to pray in those dry times of the dark night of the soul, as well as in those moments when we are especially conscious of the presence of God.

Another important fact is that we must avoid being unrealistically ambitious. If we set for ourselves a routine that will be impossible for us to follow, we will become frustrated and finally give up. It is far better to pray and meditate for ten minutes a day than to plan an hour in the morning and an hour in the evening and never get around to it. We should begin modestly, settle into a system that works, and then gradually expand it as we begin to grow and develop. It should be said, however, that we must commit a reasonable amount of time if we expect any significant deepening to occur. How much time will depend upon the individual, but it should be long enough for us to withdraw from the normal activities of the day.

The most desirable situation would be to engage in devotional activity at approximately the same times and places each day. That way it becomes as integral a part of our life as eating, sleeping, and working. There is no one right time for every person. Some of us are morning people and some of us are night people. In the morning the mind is clear and alert, the business of the day has not yet cluttered our lives, and the world is usually quieter. At night the day's work is over and will not resume until tomorrow. Many of our immediate problems are behind us, and we are free to focus on other things. For most of us, conditions will rarely be ideal and we will have to do the best we can. Generally, however, we find a way to do those things that we most want to do in life.

A regular time of devotional activity gives us a framework in which to pray and frees us from having to make decisions so that we can move on ahead. The suggestions that follow should be regarded only as an example of possible approaches. You may be able to develop something that works far better for you than any of these ideas. These suggestions are presented only as ways to get started if you have no other plans of your own.

We should begin with some kind of introductory prayer. A traditional doxology would be appropriate or a verse from the Psalms such as:

> O God, do not be far from me:
>> O my God, make haste to help me!
>>> Psalm 71:12

> Hear my cry, O God,
>> listen to my prayer.
>>> Psalm 61:1

> Be merciful to me, O God, be merciful
>> to me
> for in you my soul takes refuge.
>>> Psalm 57:1

> Make me to know your ways, O Lord;
>> teach me your paths.
> Lead me in your truth, and teach me,
>> for you are the God of my salvation;
>> for you I wait all day long.
>>> Psalm 25:4-5

Having expressed our intentions we should next try to be quiet and let our minds calm. We should attempt to free ourselves of interior distractions as much as possible and turn our attention to God. We might repeat the Jesus Prayer or a short verse of scripture until we begin to calm. We can use this silence to express our love for God on the deepest level possible, an expression that will ultimately be nonverbal.

Next we might move into some kind of directed prayer. Following centuries of Christian contemplative tradition I would recommend reading the Psalms on a daily basis and using them as our prayer. If we begin with Psalm 1 and read and pray six each day, we will cover the entire Psalter in less than a month. This includes treating each of the twenty-two sections of Psalm 119 as a separate psalm. Some basic knowledge of the history of Israel is required to understand the Psalms, but in time, as we pray them over and over, they will become our own prayers and will speak ever more profoundly to our deepest religious needs.

Equally important should be regular readings from the Gospels. Meditation on the life of Christ has already been discussed. A knowledge of Jesus' life and work is fundamental to the building of our own relationship with our Lord.

It must be emphasized that what we are talking about here is devotional reading, not merely study. Study is important in our religious growth. We must know all we can about our Christian heritage through the study of the Bible, the history of the church, and Christian theology. Intellectual discipline is an important foundation for devotional life and should not be neglected. All learning is important to the Christian, for the greater our understanding of the world and its people, the better prepared we are to probe the mysteries of life and God. Here, however, we are thinking in terms of meditation on the Psalms and the life of Jesus as a means of deepening our love for God.

A good devotional regimen must include an honest examination of conscience. We must do this in a full awareness that when we face God all of our defenses are down. Our excuses do not mean anything. Our wealth, status, appearance, or influence cannot cover our offenses against God. Painful as it might be to do, we should carefully examine the events of the past day or week and note those instances in which we have been unfaithful to God, neglected others, or violated moral commands. Only an honest awareness of our failures and imperfections can make us understand the love of

God and our absolute dependence upon divine grace and mercy.

Having done these things, we are now ready to offer prayers of petition for others and for ourselves. Recognizing the needs of people and praying for God's intervention is a responsibility of every Christian.

Ignatius of Loyola always suggested closing any time of prayer or meditation with the Lord's Prayer.

These ideas must be regarded as suggestions only. They may not work for everyone. But it is essential to engage in some kind of prayer and meditation on a regular basis. There will be days when any kind of routine will be a burden. There will be other days when it will be welcome. Sometimes we may read some scripture and not remember one word we have read. At other times we will read a word or a verse that, in a flash of insight, opens up for us a whole new world of meaning and understanding. But gradually, if we persevere, we will become conscious of a deepening faith, a more vivid awareness of God, and the truth that on God alone all things depend.

To summarize briefly, we might consider the following outline as a starting point for our time of prayer:

1. A doxology or verse from a Psalm
2. A brief period of silence for settling down, which may include repetition of the Jesus Prayer, a verse of scripture, a simple phrase, or just quiet
3. The reading of some Psalms
4. An examination of conscience
5. Prayers of petititon
6. The Lord's Prayer

As we begin to grow we will want to expand what we do. We might take an additional period in the day for meditation on something from the life of Christ or general reading. Experience will dictate what works best for us.

People have physical as well as mental capacities, and the physical side of the devotional life should not be ignored. Jesus told us to go into our rooms and close the door when we pray. He taught that people should do their fasting in secret. Christian contemplatives have noted that physical self-denial has a way of sharpening perception, although in modern times there has been a reaction against excessive mortification. How we sit or stand, however, is significant. Sloppy, lazy posture, as has already been mentioned earlier, can adversely affect our devotional efforts. What posture we use is not as important as the fact that it helps us become alert and fully aware of what we are doing. Some contemplatives today, influenced by Zen and other Eastern methods of meditation, have adopted the cross-legged lotus posture. In theory, this position produces in the body a sense of peace and well-being, especially when coupled with proper methods of breathing. Other people think they can pray better when they kneel. Most Christians at least bow their heads. There is no right or wrong posture for prayer, but it is true that the way we act physically will have some relationship to the way we act spiritually. Praying while we are reclining in bed will be a problem if we fall asleep in the middle of our prayer.

Roman Catholics make the sign of the cross when they pray. Pentecostals raise their hands above their heads. Teenagers at church camps hold hands in a "friendship circle." It is difficult to express religious feelings without some kind of physical act, however subtle it may be.

It is sometimes easier to maintain a devotional practice if we engage in some kind of outward activity. One practice that has value for some people is writing.

Keeping a spiritual diary or journal where we might write down thoughts, prayers, or insights, could be very helpful. For many years I have kept a notebook listing the Psalms read and at least one verse from each Psalm that particularly strikes me that day. It is a little thing, to be sure, but it is something I want to do each day. A minor, intermediate goal is to avoid any skipped dates or blank pages. More important, however, is the fact that a commitment to keep this kind of a journal causes you to be more careful about finding time for prayer. It also forces you to stop everything else you are doing. It is impossible to write down Psalm verses while engaging in other activity. Of course, keeping up a discipline for its own sake is not the point. The reason for doing anything like this is to enable us to live the gospel more faithfully.

A sample page from such a journal would look like this:

July 26—Psalms 46–51

"Be still and know that I am God!
　　I am exalted among the nations,
　　I am exalted in the earth."
　　　　　　　　　　　　　　　—46

God is king over the nations;
　　God sits on his holy throne.
　　　　　　　　　　　　　　　—47

We ponder your steadfast love, O God,
　　in the midst of your temple.
　　　　　　　　　　　　　　　—48

God will ransom my soul from the
　　　　power of Sheol,
　　for he will receive me.
　　　　　　　　　　　　　　　—49

Those who bring thanksgiving as their
sacrifice honor me;
to those who go the right way
I will show the salvation of God.

—50

Create in me a clean heart, O God,
and put a new and right spirit
within me.

—51

These verses are rich food for thought. Writing them
down impresses them upon the mind and they can be
thought about through the day. Month by month, as we
read through the Psalter again and again, the Psalms
become impressed upon our lives and in them we begin
to sense the presence of the God of Israel. A simple little
procedure can produce deep spiritual growth.

While the busy schedule of the average American
home may make this kind of activity difficult, there are
opportunities for prayer and meditation elsewhere that
can be used to advantage. For example, going to church
on Sunday provides us with time for prayer and meditation. Church services usually provide several periods
of time that do not require our full attention. We ought
to urge our churches to provide more. The time before
the service begins can be used for meditating on scripture, prayer, or just quiet.

Many pastors provide some time for silent prayer in
the service. The time when the offering is being received
is often relatively free from distraction. One of the
finest opportunities occurs when the Lord's Supper is
being celebrated. Communion practices vary greatly from
church to church, but in almost every case the distribu-
tion of the bread and wine requires several minutes that
can be precious to us for meditation and prayer.

But there is another aspect of praying in church that needs to be considered, and that is the necessity of communal prayer. A devotional life that is purely individualistic and seeks only personal religious experience is not faithful to the gospel. The two greatest commandments that Jesus gave us are to love God and to love other people. This requires reaching out beyond ourselves to others as well as to God. If our spiritual life says nothing about how we live together in community, it is lacking in authenticity and faithfulness. "Those who say, 'I love God,' and hate their brothers or sisters, are liars; for those who do not love a brother or sister whom they have seen, cannot love God whom they have not seen. The commandment we have from him is this: those who love God must love their brothers and sisters also" (1 John 4:20–21).

People need to stand together in acknowledging their mutual dependence on God. We need to encourage each other in the quest for religious knowledge. We need to share experiences with those who are struggling with hard questions and will not accept easy answers. We can learn much from each other in our mutual exploration of the divine mysteries.

The point of the ecumenical movement is that we are one in Christ Jesus. This also means that we can learn from each other's religious experience. If someone in a religious tradition different from our own has learned something significant about the reality of God, we ought to find out what that is. One of the bonds that unites religious people is the common desire to understand spiritual reality, and we can profit richly from sharing what we have experienced. This is an aspect of our oneness in Christ. Our common experience of spiritual reality creates bonds that can never be broken. So we worship God, we praise and pray, and we commune together, for we are all children of God and we would all know the one from whom life came.

Having said that, I would still affirm the advantage of temporary withdrawal from the normal routine and associations of life. Somehow, we must find ways in our society for people to retreat from their normal surroundings and look at life from a different perspective. We need to take significant blocks of time, several days at least, for withdrawal and retreat in order to devote ourselves fully to our quest for God. We will return to the normal routine greatly enriched and renewed.

There are churches, denominations, and organizations that provide retreat opportunities. We ought to take advantage of them and encourage them. On a retreat of several days we can accomplish more than we could in a whole year of trying to squeeze a heavy amount of devotional activity into a daily schedule that is already overcrowded. A retreat is not a substitute for regular prayer, but it is a supplement that can help us take giant steps forward.

Under the most ideal conditions, a retreat should be carried out under the guidance of a competent spiritual director. While private retreats are useful, a retreat with a group where a common schedule is followed and the fulfillment of a common purpose is sought will give us encouragement and guidance in using our time.

A major element in a good retreat will be silence. We should avoid the distraction of conversation for a few days as far as possible. There ought to be places where we can be alone and not worry about other people watching us or making judgments about us.

A schedule of devotional activity will help to guarantee that we use our time to the best advantage. For example, we might set one period of the day for examination of conscience, another for meditation, another for reading, and others for various types of prayer. Periods of instruction and counsel by a spiritual director will save us from many pitfalls.

The emphasis on such a retreat should not be fellowship, recreation, or entertainment, even though some of these might be good by-products. The main emphasis should be on spiritual development, a seeking after God, and the cleansing of self. If such a retreat were successful, it would build up our faith, increase our love for God, and develop a new openness and depth of compassion toward other people.

It is important to go on a religious retreat with an open mind. I have seen retreats fail with college students because some of them made up their minds what the retreat should accomplish even before it started. When things didn't work out that way they became frustrated. Having expected to be fed they went home starving. It is far better to make tentative plans about what we will do, and then just let whatever happens happen. Turn it all over to God. With such an open attitude our retreat might actually prove more valuable than if it had accomplished what we originally thought we wanted. We cannot predict what the Spirit will do or where it will lead us, but we must be free to follow it and to trust it.

Can a retreat be a family affair? It can if all members of the family agree on the purpose and are willing to follow the discipline of it. Otherwise, those who want something other than spiritual development will be a serious hindrance, even though they might not intend to be. In a good retreat we must be free to find solitude and silence, and the people with whom we are making a retreat must respect those needs. No retreat situation will be ideal, of course, but we must seek opportunities for brief withdrawal into the desert where we can pursue our quest for God. Such a temporary withdrawal will have a significant effect on the way we live our lives in the world.

Reading has already been mentioned as an important tool of the devotional life. We should always have a reading project under way, even if we can only read a few pages a day much of the time. There is a wide variety of devotional material available today, and people of almost any reading and intellectual level should be able to find something suitable. The best devotional books are those written by people who have been through the desert, who have struggled with the dark night of the soul, and, in the process, have been able to sense the reality of God on the deepest levels. They have the most of teach us.

Some of the best Christian devotional writing comes from the ancient and medieval periods of Christian history. The works of Augustine, Bernard of Clairvaux, Henry Suso, Meister Eckhart, Bonaventure, the unknown authors of *The Cloud of Unknowing* and *The Imitation of Christ*, just to mention a few of the people referred to in this book, will surprise us with their contemporary relevance. Some of these writers are not easy to read, but we should not let the struggle deter us from spiritual growth. The basic problems of Christian people, as far as the spiritual life is concerned, are the same in every age: the obscurity of God, the satisfaction of deep religious longings, the distractions that cloud our vision of the divine mysteries. The great spiritual writers faced these problems, and we can learn much from them.

There are, of course, many excellent spiritual writers from other periods of Christian history. From more recent centuries we have Martin Luther, Ignatius of Loyola, John of the Cross, John Wesley, George Fox,

Rufus Jones, John Woolman, John Baille, Thomas Kelly, Evelyn Underhill, Thomas Merton, Henry Nouwen, Basil Pennington, as well as many others who have something of substance to contribute to our spiritual development that rises above a superficial popular piety.

Many churches and denominations publish monthly or quarterly devotional books that provide us with daily Bible readings, material for meditation, and prayers. These can give us a basic structure for our prayer life from which we can move as deeply as we wish.

In addition to devotional and mystical classics, we also ought to read solid books on Christian theology. The theological giants of our century have attempted to organize Christian theology systematically so we can sort out both the problems and the resources. The Christian religion faces many hard questions today, especially in the development of modern science, what we are learning from psychology, and cultural interaction. We must not avoid questions because they are hard. Our faith will grow as we struggle to come to terms with difficult questions. We must remember that when we are dealing with theological issues we are not engaging in abstract intellectual exercises; we are dealing with our status before God and our understanding of transcendence. This kind of reading will keep our minds active and alert as we ponder the mystery of God.

Seeing

7

Give justice to the weak
and the orphan;
Maintain the right of the
lowly and the destitute.

Psalm 82:3

Thus far, we have been considering a style of spirituality that is largely private and interior. While many Christians are attracted to this approach, some will have difficulty with it. Outgoing, highly extroverted people are often frustrated with silence and solitude and must approach religion in other ways.

There is value, of course, in developing the opposite side of our personality tendencies. If we are highly extroverted we should try to develop our interior life. If we are introverted, we need to work on our relationships with the outside world. Still, the style of spirituality we practice will be determined by the kind of personality

we have. In this chapter, we will consider an approach
to the spiritual life that is different from what we have
pondered up to this point.

There is an approach that says that we can find God
in other people and in what is happening in the world.
The biblical tradition teaches us that we are all created
in the image of God. Each of us, in some sense, is a
revelation of God. To be sure, that image is obscured to
a greater or lesser degree in every person, but that
image is there.

Those who follow this approach in their search for
God rely heavily on the parable of the last judgment in
Matthew 25. We are given a magnificent picture of
Christ sitting on a throne of glory, surrounded by
angels, with all of the nations gathered before him. The
time has come for him to judge, to separate those who
will enter the Kingdom from those who won't.
What was his standard of judgment? It was not faithfulness to religious law, it was not believing correct
doctrine, it was not even church attendance. It was
whether people had fed the hungry, given a drink to the
thirsty, welcomed the stranger, clothed the naked,
cared for the sick, and visited the prisoner. Those who
had done such things had done them to him, Jesus told
his mystified disciples. "Just as you did it to one of the
least of these who are members of my family, you did it
to me."

Who are members of the family of Jesus? The disciples, all of his followers, his ethnic family, the family
of God, all people created in God's image?

The point is that when we do something to or for
someone else, we may be doing it to Christ. When we
neglect another person who crosses our path, we may be
neglecting Christ. What would it do to human relationships if we all saw Christ in each other?

I would like to mention two people from our own century whose spirituality was based on the assumption that Christ is present in other people, and that is where we can find him.

Dorothy Day has been regarded by many people as one of the saints of our time. She was born in 1897, the daughter of a journalist. Eventually she chose that profession for herself and, early in her career, wrote for various radical newspapers in New York. Although she was not brought up in the church, she had some deep religious yearnings that surfaced from time to time. The culture in which she moved was hostile to religion, but she had a sense that something was not right with her life. When her child from a common law marriage was born, Dorothy had her baptized. A few months later she herself was baptized in the Roman Catholic Church.

While covering the hunger march in Washington during the depression for a Catholic magazine, she prayed that God might show her how to do something worthwhile with her life. The prayer was answered when she met a man named Peter Maurin, He was convinced that world problems could be solved if people would apply the ethics of Jesus to the problems of society.

Together, Dorothy Day and Peter Maurin began the Catholic Worker. It consisted of several programs. Most visible was a monthly newspaper called *The Catholic Worker* that published articles on various social ills and how the Christian ethic could resolve them. They also organized a Catholic Worker house, which they called a house of hospitality. It provided food and clothing for street people in New York.

Visitors to the house included alcoholics, drug addicts, the insane, and sometimes violent people. The staff often had to break up fights, but no one was turned away. Dorothy Day said that whenever you give food to another person, you are giving it to Christ, and she believed that Christ was present in every person.

This was not an easy life she had chosen. She was fond of quoting Father Zossima in *The Brothers Karamazov* who said, "Love in practice is a harsh and dreadful thing compared to love in dreams." She said in one of her newspaper columns, "It is hard to see the dear sweet Christ in many a pestering drunk that comes in demanding attention." But she was convinced that even such people were "God's messengers." People, she believed, could see Christ in each other if they were sensitive enough. God was incarnate in the poor, and she saw that as they ate meals together in the Catholic Worker house. Like the disciples on the road to Emmaus, Dorothy Day saw Christ revealed in the breaking of bread.

Day also had an interior spirituality. She said that prayer was as necessary to life as breathing. She prayed the Psalms morning and evening as well as the Lord's Prayer three times a day. She said that the Jesus Prayer was helpful to her in stressful situations.

The dominant characteristic of her spirituality, however, was her dedication to the poor. That is where she found Christ. She lived a life of voluntary poverty. She had no salary. Her work depended entirely on the charity of others. But, somehow, there was always enough.

At her funeral in New York the pallbearers were carrying her pine box into the church when an obviously demented person moved to the casket and stared at it with great intensity. No one stopped the man because it was in the wretched of the earth that Dorothy Day saw God.

Dom Helder Camara retired as a Brazilian archbishop. During his career he was known for a deep spirituality, yet he was a strong advocate for third world economic development. He was critical of those political and economic structures that deliberately kept people in poverty.

Camara was born in a poor area in northeastern Brazil, also the child of a journalist. Entering the priesthood, he developed expertise in the field of education and rapidly rose through the ranks of the clergy. Early in his career he felt that a strong, dictatorial government was the only way to maintain law and order in society. Later, however, he became deeply concerned about the poor who were exploited through structures over which they had no control. Eventually, he became Archbishop of Olinda and Recife, his home area, where he dedicated himself to alleviating the problems of the poor.

He adopted a simple lifestyle, living in a small room in a church rather than the episcopal palace. There are stories about his presenting himself at the police station with bag packed, offering to trade himself for prisoners he knew had been unjustly arrested. Because of his concern for the poor, the government would not allow the media to report on his life.

Camara was a man of deep prayer. His routine was to get up at 2:00 a.m., pray for two hours, and then go back to bed. That was the only way he could schedule serious prayer in his very busy life. He said that if he did not pray regularly, he would find himself depleted and would have nothing to offer to God or other people.

Like Dorothy Day, Dom Helder Camara believed that Christ could be found in other people. "Christ in the North-East," Camara said, "is called Jose, Antonio, Severino. This is Christ, the name who needs justice, who has a right to justice, who deserves justice." He had no doubt that Christ was present in the poor. When people complained to him that he could not see Christ in an unemployed drunk, Camara had an answer. When people are forced to live in subhuman conditions, as he believed that two-thirds of people of the world live, they become like animals. But when you see them up close, said Camara, you see the face of Christ. Jesus was reduced to a subhuman condition on the cross.

There is no problem with hearing the voice of God today, the Archbishop believed. It can be heard in the voices of those who suffer injustice. He reminded people that we shall be judged by how we have treated Christ, the Christ who is hungry and thirsty, dirty, injured, and oppressed.

These are two examples of a spirituality that finds Christ outside the self. While both Day and Camara practiced solitary prayer and developed their interior lives, they put heavy emphasis on seeing God in other people. They took that parable of the last judgment seriously, giving their lives to helping people because they knew they would be doing it to Christ.

While these two people gave themselves to the service of the poor, we must keep in mind that suffering knows no economic boundaries. There is a sense in which the Christ in us is crucified again whenever we suffer. When human relationships are broken and people are alienated from each other, the crucifixion takes place again. Whenever people starve and die from hunger and thirst, the crucifixion takes place again. Whenever people suffer from mental and emotional illness, Christ is crucified in our midst. Whenever the innocent in war lose everything, even their lives, Christ is crucified. Whenever we mistreat another human being, we crucify the Christ in that person. All over this planet the circumstances of life cause many to cry out, "My God, my God, why have you forsaken me?" We are painfully aware that in many places on the earth people cry out with Jesus, "I am thirsty."

This is a powerful spirituality, one that calls us to be attentive to the presence of God in other people's lives. But if we were to relate to them as if they were Christ, what a difference it would make in human relationships.

This is not an easy kind of spirituality. It requires what Dorothy Day called a harsh and dreadful love. It is incredibly difficult to see Christ in some people, but that is the challenge of the parable of the last judgment.

Putting It All Together   8

Let them thank the LORD for his
steadfast love,
for his wonderful works to
humankind.
For he satisfies the thirsty,
and the hungry he fills with good
things.

Psalm 107:8–9

The title of this book is misleading, for it implies that the "spiritual life" is something different and apart from our normal existence. The term has been used only to describe a particular kind of activity, and should not be regarded as something divorced for the ordinary pursuits of living in the world. The active and contemplative lives are not opposites, for a well-balanced Christian life includes both action and contemplation. The neglect of either distorts what life should be. Furthermore, dividing the world into spiritual and secular realms is to create a false division. What we might call our spiritual experience influences all of the activity of our lives, often unconsciously, and any understanding of the world that ignores the sovereignty to God does not understand the true nature of reality, that it is God's creation. Our "spiritual lives," then, are intimately related to our jobs, our families, and our community life, for they help determine who we are. We do not consciously have to make a connection between our spirituality and our lives in the world. It is already there. If our devotional life has any degree of seriousness about it, it will be a determining factor in our lifestyles.

In his excellent book, *The Art of Loving*, Eric Fromm, a psychoanalyst, said that the deepest need of humanity is to overcome separateness and loneliness. Fromm's thesis is that this can be done only through love. Christianity says to people who feel helpless and at the mercy of forces they cannot control that they are loved, in the fullest sense of the word, by that Transcendent Power which is sovereign over all things. But Jesus also taught that we are what God intended us to be when we love God and other people. The final aim of the spiritual life is to achieve a sense of union with God. The most essential element in this effort is not method; it is the ability to love. It is in loving and being loved that our loneliness is overcome.

We begin with those kinds of love that seem most natural to us and move from there toward loving God. Our love for our wives or husbands, our children, our parents, and our friends teaches us the nature of love itself. We must love what we can see before we are able to love what we cannot see. It is this love that makes possible the establishment of a living relationship with God. On this foundation we can begin building a spiritual life. This means that all our relationships are religiously significant. Our capacity to relate to God is inseparably connected to our capacity to relate to others. We must be capable of loving and receiving love from people if we would love God and understand God's love for persons.

Thomas Merton said that the purpose of the individual life is to be a place in which God has chosen to be present. We must see ourselves as persons in whom God is present and through whom God will be known to people. Prayer and meditation and the other spiritual disciplines serve to make us more consciously aware of our status as creatures of God, people whom God has made, whom God knows, and through whom God works in the world. Arriving at this understanding requires a penetration into our selfhood at a far deeper level than that on which we normally operate.

If God is present in us, God is also present in other people. One way we relate to God is through human encounters. If people are indeed made in the image of God, then we can search for God in our relationships with each other. Sometimes it is easy to see God in other people; sometimes it is almost impossible. But every individual contains the divine image, no matter how badly obscured it may be by sin, selfishness, anger, hostility, or any other barrier that separates us.

We see this image of God when people do acts of mercy; we see it when people reach out in love; we see it when someone accepts us in spite of our imperfections. Throughout the experiences of the day, the image of God shows itself to us.

So we do not find God only in solitude and quiet. I am convinced that we do need periodic withdrawal, even if only a few minutes a day, to refocus our attention on God. But a true contemplative seeks and recognizes the presence of God in the normal activities of life, especially in interaction with others. In beauty, in nature, in the innocence of children, in the working out of justice in history, in countless ways, we discern the presence of God. This kind of discernment begins to develop when we have trained and conditioned ourselves to be open to the presence of God.

Our activity in the world, then, cannot be regarded as a distraction that retards our spiritual development. Busy family life may make it difficult to find time for silence and prayer, but family life does provide a context in which we can explore and express love. Most of the jobs we have require some degree of relating to other people. These contacts can be seen as barriers to the spiritual life, or they can be seen as opportunities for developing the capacity for love. This cannot be approached naively, however, There are some human relationships that are just plain difficult. Competition in business leads some people to regard others with suspicion. Personnel managers have problems with unproductive employees, and workers sometimes suffer under unreasonable superiors. Rivalry and ambition create barriers between individuals. No matter how hard we try to establish positive relationships, sometimes it will not work.

Such situations may seem hopeless, but they do serve to convict us of our spiritual poverty. They make us all too keenly aware that we cannot make the world what we think it should be by our own efforts. They point up our need for grace, mercy, and love. So we can learn from all sides of life. Every condition in which we find ourselves can contribute something to our spiritual growth.

A number of years ago a prominent social activist expressed concern that Christians had begun to turn away from the great issues of the day to retreat into what he called "the pygmy world of private piety." Such a conception is a distortion of the spiritual life. Prayer should never be used to escape from the problems of the world. On the contrary, the kinds of practices described in this book should produce a greater understanding of the world as the arena of God's activity and a stronger identification with human problems. The spiritual life is not an escape; it is a source of direction and strength for living and working responsibly in the world. It is a means of clarifying our perception of what is really happening.

A strong devotional life is essential to social action that has any lasting effect. After all, how can we serve God in the world if we really do not know God? But more important, the kind of interior discipline discussed in these chapters helps us to see human problems on a deeper level, preventing us from being too naive about their solutions. We need to take evil more seriously than we do, for it is not something that can be solved just by institutional programs, restructuring society, or good will. We face something more powerful than that.

I have a good friend who used to live in a small experimental monastery not far from my home. A few years ago this man, who spent several hours a day in prayer, decided to walk to Washington, D.C., on a pilgrimage for peace. He wanted to let people know that a monk, normally hidden from the world, felt strongly about peace. After he returned from his 225-mile walk he sent around a newsletter in which he recounted his experience. He told of one instance when he was attacked by a dog. He kicked the dog so hard that it was stunned. Then he realized that this kind of violence was ironic on a walk for peace.

He told me that he did a lot of thinking about that incident and realized that violence is not just an act of will, it is something woven into the very fabric of our humanity. It is a mystery, an evil influence that is part of each of us. It takes more than good intentions to overcome it, and my friend spoke of it as one of those demons that can only be driven out by prayer and fasting. A person of prayer sees things differently. Violence is not a problem to be solved by passing another law. It is a deep spiritual problem, and we must understand this if we would try to deal with it effectively.

This is what the spiritual life is all about: seeing things on another level, getting below the surface appearance of the world to the deeper levels of reality, a level that a shallow-thinking person never knows.

One of the dangers of reading the Bible is that we may be rudely shaken out of our complacency. The Psalms are filled with social concern. God is described in them as one who will finally act for the benefit of widows, orphans, prisoners, the hungry, the oppressed, the suffering innocents, and the poor. In Matthew 25 Jesus said that those who survive the last judgment will be those who fed the hungry, gave drink to the thirsty, welcomed the stranger, clothed the naked, and visited prisoners and the sick. It is a hard thing to live by the Christian ethic, and we cannot do it without a generous measure of grace. An intentional devotional life will help us to understand both the ethic and the grace. It will awaken us to what God wants for the world and will lead us to those undergirding spiritual resources that enable us to work at it.

It is sometimes said by spiritual writers that people who talk the most about the spiritual life are those who do not have one. Perhaps that is because such people see the spiritual life as something unique and separate from ordinary existence. In fact, those most deeply into it probably do not talk about it as something special because it is such an integral part of their living. They just live it. They work from day to day, knowing that they live in the presence of God and under God's sovereignty. Having tasted and seen that the Lord is good, they go on their way, sharing the love of God in all of the common pursuits of life.

It is tempting to become interested in prayer because of what it might do for us. We hope that through it a sick friend might be healed, a broken family reunited, and failure changed into success. Sometimes motivation might be considerably less than that. There might be a hope that a business will prosper, the stock market go up, or a game won. There are also those who take up prayer in the hope that it will turn them on to a spiritual high or that it will produce a warm cozy feeling inside.

The best prayer is probably prayer that on the surface would seem to be useless: simple praise, an expression of love, a cry of thanksgiving. The apostle Paul told the Corinthians that the gospel was folly. It really made no sense. The cross was a stumbling block because the Son of God could not save himself. It may well be that a life of prayer will bring about no material improvement in our lives. It is no guarantee against tragedy or misery. Prayer tends to lose its essential character when it is used to achieve some material purpose. As Bernard of Clairvaux said, the only reason to love God is God.

There seems to be a common element in all mystical religion, whether Christian or any other variety, and that is an awareness that all is one. There is nothing in our lives unrelated to God.

God is the source of all that is and sovereign over all things.

There is not a single action of the day that cannot be related in some way to our experience with God. We ought to offer to God every morning our thoughts, our words, and our actions, and renew this intention throughout the day. Each day we have is a gift from God, and to live apart from the giver is not only an illusion, it is to violate the intention and harmony of creation. So let us direct our lives toward God that we might taste and see that the Lord is good.

Bibliography

This book is based on some major classics in the literature of Christian spirituality. Below are listed the authors mentioned in the text and on whose work the book is heavily based. Any bookstore will have a copy of *Books in Print* where you can look up a listing of their writings and the various editions available.

Augustine
Bonaventure
Bonhoeffer, Dietrich
Calvin, John
Camara, Dom Helder
The Cloud of Unknowing
Day, Dorothy

Eckhart, Meister
Ignatius of Loyola
John of the Cross
Luther, Martin
Merton, Thomas
Suso, Henry
Wesley, John

The Paulist Press (997 Macarthur Boulevard, Mahwah, New Jersey 07430) is publishing a series of books called Classics of Western Spirituality. It includes new translations and editions of the major Christian classics as well as works by Moslem, Jewish, and Native American writers. A catalog of titles is available. Paperback editions of many of the classics are also available from Doubleday Image Books (666 Fifth Avenue, New York, NY 10103).

The following list comprises recommendations for a basic libary of books on Christian spirituality. These are not intended for devotional reading, but for studying the history and theology of the tradition.

Bouyer, Louis and others, *A History of Christian Spirituality*. Three Volumes. New York: Seabury Press, 1982.

Christian Spirituality. New York: Crossroad, 1985-1991. Three volumes have appeared so far. Each contains essays on various aspects of Christian spirituality in different historical periods. The volumes are part of a larger series called *World Spirituality: An Encyclopedic History of the Religious Quest.*

Cox, Michael, *Handbook of Christian Spirituality: The Major Figures and Teachings from the New Testament to the 20th Century.* San Francisco: Harper and Row, 1985. A concise survey of the literature of Christian spirituality.

Holmes, Urban T., III, *A History of Christian Spirituality: An Analytical Introduction.* San Francisco: Harper and Row, 1981.

Jones, Cheslyn, Geoffrey Wainwright, and Edward Yarnold, editors, *The Study of Sprirituality.* New York: Oxford University Press, 1986. A major collection of essays on various aspects of Christian spirituality.

Jungmann, Josef A., *Christian Prayer Through the Centuries.* New York: Paulist Press, 1978.

Kepler, Thomas S., editor, *An Anthology of Devotional Literature.* Grand Rapids: Baker Book House, 1977. This book was published earlier under the title *The Fellowship of the Saints.* It includes selections from writers from the first century through the middle of the twentieth century.

Knowles, David, *What Is Mysticism?* London: Sheed and Ward, 1966.

Magill, Frank N. and Iam P. McGreal, editors, *Christian Spirituality: The Essential Guide to the Most Influential Spiritual Writings of the Christian Tradition.* San Francisco: Harper and Row, 1988. Contains summaries of many of the classics and contemporary books as well as biographical information on the authors. A useful tool for those who want to see the possibilities for study.

Senn, Frank C., editor, *Protestant Spiritual Traditions.* New York: Paulist Press, 1986.

Underhill, Evelyn, *Mysticism.* New York: Doubleday Image Books, 1990. (First published in 1911.)

Wakefield, Gordon S., *The Westminister Dictionary of Christian Spirituality.* Philadelphia: Westminster Press, 1983.

I am frequently asked to recommend devotional reading for people. That is a difficult task, for people have different reading levels and interests. How do we distinguish between the popular and superficial and that which has real substance to it? The following list probably represents my own taste more than anything else. I find the most value in reading the work of those who have been through a serious spiritual struggle, who have recognized that probing mystery is not easy, and that spiritual growth and the knowledge of God cannot be oversimplified. I also reject that which tends to trivialize faith by not recognizing the power of evil, the realities of dry periods in the spiritual life, and the fact that we have more questions than we have answers. Having said that, let me list some of the books I have found most helpful. Most of the writers have produced a number of books. I will not list them all, but a few examples. You may want to read others.

Bloom, Anthony, *Beginning to Pray.* New York: Paulist Press, 1982. Bloom is a physician who became a Russian Orthodox bishop. See also, among others, *Living Prayer* (Springfield, Illinois: Templegate Publishers, 1966).

Brown, Robert McAfee, *Spirituality and Liberation: Overcoming the Great Fallacy.* Philadelphia: Westminster Press, 1988.

Doherty, Catherine de Hueck, *Poustinia*. Notre Dame, Indiana: Ave Maria Press, 1975. A very interesting book about solitude, written from the Russian Orthodox perspective. See also her *Strannik: The Call to Pilgrimage for Western Man* (Notre Dame, Indiana: Ave Maria Press, 1988).

Foster, Richard J., *Celebration of Discipline: The Path to Spiritual Growth*. San Francisco: Harper and Row, 1988.

Hammarskjold, Dag, *Markings*. New York: Alfred A. Knopf, 1964.

Johnston, William, *Christian Mysticism Today*. San Francisco: Harper and Row, 1984. Johnston has an interest in studying the relationship of the spirituality of the East and the West, especially Zen Buddhism and Christianity. See also his *The Inner Eye of Love: Mysticism and Religion* (San Francisco: Harper and Row, 1978). See also *The Still Point: Reflections on Zen and Christian Mysticism*, *Christian Zen*, *Silent Music*, and *The Mirror Mind: Spirituality and Transformation*.

Kelsey, Morton T., *The Other Side of Silence: A Guide to Christian Meditation*. New York: Paulist Press, 1976. See also *Encounter with God* (Minneapolis: Bethany Fellowship, 1972), *Companions on the Inner Way: The Art of Spiritual Guidance* (New York: Crossroad, 1983), and *Adventure Inward: Christian Growth Through Personal Journal Writing* (Minneapolis: Augsburg, 1980).

Leech, Kenneth, *Experiencing God: Theology as Spirituality*. San Francisco: HarperCollins, 1989. See also his earlier book, *Soul Friend: The Practice of Christian Spirituality* (San Francisco: Harper and Row, 1980).

Maloney, George A., *Prayer of the Heart*. Notre Dame,

Indiana: Ave Maria Press, 1981.

Merton, Thomas, *New Seeds of Contemplation*. New York: New Directions, 1972. Merton was one of the most popular and influential spiritual writers in the twentieth century. His autobiography, *The Seven Story Mountain*, describes his pilgrimage that eventually led him into the life of a Trappist monk. Other good books by Merton include *Contemplative Prayer* (Garden City, New York: Doubleday, 1971); *Conjectures of a Guilty Bystander* (Garden City, NY: Doubleday, 1968); *Life and Holiness* (Garden City, NY: Doubleday, 1969); *Mystics and Zen Masters* (New York: Farrar, Straus and Giroux, 1986); and *Thoughts in Solitude* (New York: Farrar, Straus and Giroux, 1976). Some readers might have an interest in *The Collected Poems of Thomas Merton* (New York: New Directions, 1980).

Nouwen, Henri J. M., *Reaching Out: The Three Movements of the Spiritual Life*. Garden City, New York: Doubleday, 1986. Nouwen is a popular spiritual writer. Among his other books is *The Living Reminder: Service and Prayer in Memory of Jesus Christ* (San Francisco: Harper and Row 1984), a fine book about ministry.

Pennington, M. Basil, *Centering Prayer: Renewing an Ancient Christian Prayer Form*. Garden City, New York: Doubleday, 1982. Pennington is a Trappist monk. See also *A Place Apart: Monastic Prayer and Practice for Everyone* (Garden City, New York: Doubleday, 1985) and *Call to the Center: The Gospel's Invitation to Deeper Prayer* (New York: Doubleday, 1990).

Reinhold, H. A., *The Soul Afire: Revelations of the Mystics*. Garden City, New York: Doubleday, 1973.

Underhill, Evelyn, *Practical Mysticism*. Ohio: Canal

Winchester, Ariel, 1986. Underhill was a popular and influential British spiritual writer in the first half of this century. Her books continue to be reprinted. In addition to *Mysticism*, mentioned above, other good books by her include *The House of the Soul and Concerning the Inner Life* (Minneapolis: Metheun and Company, Ltd, 1947), and *the Life of the Spirit and the Life of Today* (San Francisco: Harper and Row, 1986).

The Way of a Pilgrim. Translated by R. M. French. New York: Seabury Press, 1965.

Finally, what are some good guides for daily prayer? There are many possibilities. Some people are attracted to the Roman Catholic breviary, which arranges the Psalms and other items to be prayed in the morning, at midday, in the evening, and at night. There are many editions available, including some abbreviated versions that have only morning and evening prayer.

Protestant publications include the following:

The Book of Common Prayer of the Episcopal Church. It includes liturgies for morning, noonday, evening prayer, and compline. There are several editions available.

Job, Rueben P. and Norman Shawchuck, *A Guide for Ministers and Other Servants.* Nashville: The Upper Room, 1983. This book is set up on a weekly basis, offering an invocation, a Psalm, readings, prayers, a hymn, and benediction. In addition, there are scripture readings for each day of the week. There are also outlines for monthly retreats.

Kinnamon, Katherine and Michael Kinnamon, *Every Day We Will Bless You.* St. Louis: Chalice Press, 1990. For each day there is an invocation, a Psalm, a scripture reading, and suggestions for prayer.